MW01153082

Fine CHOCOLATES
Great EXPERIENCE 3

EXTENDING SHELF LIFE

Jean-Pierre Wybauw

PHOTOGRAPHY **FRANK CROES**

TABLE OF CONTENTS

FOREWORD

As a result of our improved knowledge of what is good and bad with respect to food, people are living healthier lifestyles with increased awareness, which is a positive development. Especially the knowledge that the use of fats and sugars could be harmful to our health encourages us to reflect about our consumption habits. The list of ingredients on food packaging is often thoroughly examined before these products are purchased. For example, savvy consumers are increasingly limiting the ingredients that are harmful to their health, and think twice before being tempted by desserts and confectionery in general.

Our profession as producers of pralines is also undergoing a massive development process. Labour is getting increasingly expensive and we are therefore forced to work more efficiently by producing larger quantities, which eventually will save us time. Instead of producing a small quantity of pralines each week, we produce more in a shorter period of time allowing us to get by longer. In addition, we are faced with fierce competition, which is why we target other sales markets and venture into export. All this implies that our products must have longer shelf life. This development results in a dilemma: on the one hand we strive for long shelf life and on the other hand, for high-quality recipes with superior ingredients. However, it is precisely these high-quality ingredients, such as cream and butter, which have limited shelf life due to their high water content. The shorter the time between a praline's production and its consumption, the better. The fresher the product, the better it tastes. As the product gets older, the flavour of the filling and the chocolate will tend to blend. The chocolate's structure will also be influenced by the filling, especially in chocolates containing a lot of fats.

These days our products must travel a long way before ending up in the hands of consumers and we are forced to adjust our recipes. In the meantime technology obviously does not stand still. The industries that supply the ingredients are also in constant development. The time of the traditional recipes exclusively made from butter, cream and fondant – for that matter very sweet, greasy and rich – is long gone.

In order to keep up with the times and to be able to create recipes with longer shelf life the modern chocolatier must have a broader basic knowledge of the ingredients, enabling them to make fewer unconscious errors in the recipes and processing methods and as a result stand a better chance of retaining their clientele. Due to the aforementioned development, I found it useful to write a book about the shelf life of pralines and its potential extension. Nonetheless I still prefer the earlier scenario with simple recipes and short best-by dates after production. In this book I have attempted to shed some light on the current knowledge of ingredients and to describe in an easy-to-understand language how to best process said ingredients.

Lastly, I would like to emphasise that this book is far from complete and will never be, since science and techniques in our profession constantly evolve.

Jean-Pierre Wybauw

ABOUT THE AUTHOR

Jean-Pierre Wybauw has authored the books *Fine Chocolates 1, Chocolate without borders, Chocolate Decorations, Fine Chocolates 2 – Great Ganache Experience* and *¡Chocolate Foodie!*

Jean-Pierre studied at the Centre for Instruction and Research in the Food Industries COOVI-CERIA in Brussels. He also earned a diploma in specialised decoration techniques, desserts and marzipan figurines at the PIVA patisserie school in Antwerp.

He began his career in the world of patisserie. Subsequently he became chocolatier at Del Rey, Antwerp's most renowned confectioners, where he was promoted to head of the design department. He went on to become a full-time teacher in confectionaries (day and evening classes) at the COOVI-CERIA for seven years. In 1965 he created the first transfer foils to print on chocolate, which is currently used worldwide. Between 1965 and 1974 he was a well-known contributor to various culinary magazines. In 1972, after these exciting years, Jean-Pierre started working in the Callebaut chocolate factory in Lebbeke-Wieze (B) as technical adviser and head of the demonstration department.

In his spare time he also travels the world to conduct courses, deliver lectures and hold demonstrations in chocolate processing. He is, for example, a regular guest lecturer at the Culinary Institute of America in Greystone, CA and Hyde Park, NY, the French Pastry School in Chicago, the Notterschool in Florida, the Savour school in Victoria, Australia, L'école Olivier Bajard in France, the World Pastry Forum in Las Vegas and Phoenix, the ZDS Fachschule in Solingen, etc. In 1990 he became a member of the International Richemont Club. He is furthermore often invited as a guest on foreign television cookery programmes and is also a well-known and respected member of the jury in numerous competitions. His expert opinion on working with chocolate is especially appreciated in international competitions, as in Beaver Creek, USA, the biennial World Championship in Las Vegas and Phoenix, the Oskar in Vienna, etc.

Jean-Pierre Wybauw won numerous distinctions and competitions, such as, for example, in 2002, the coveted title of 'Chef of the year' at the Culinary Institute of America in Hyde Park, NY. He also won gold in Australia with his successful book *Fine Chocolates – Great Experience 1* for the 'World Food Media Award 2006' in the category 'Best Professional Cookbook'. In the meantime the book has been translated into seven languages. Its French and English version have also earned first prize with the 'Gourmand World Cookbook Awards' in Malaysia as 'best technical chocolate book in the world'. Two years later he was the only chef to earn the special 'Gourmand Award Best of the Best' in Frankfurt, where the winners were selected from Gourmand Awards from the past eight years.

During his successful career he also studied painting techniques at the Academy of Fine Arts in Antwerp and Kontich and his works are being exhibited at this time in a number of galleries. Currently Jean-Pierre Wybauw is active as an international chocolate and sugar processing consultant.

OUR RESPONSIBILITY
AS PRODUCERS

INTRODUCTION

What aspects contribute to the creation of the perfectly flavoured finished article?
Despite all efforts made, consumers may still notice flavour deviations in the finished product, which may be the result of reactions taking place between the product's production and itsconsumption. Chocolate products are seldom consumed immediately after production. It is therefore clear that the negative flavour changes, which may occur between production and consumption, must be reduced to an absolute minimum as food incidents may represent risks to customers. That is why it has to be rapidly clear what the reason is. In order to comply with the rising need for insight and safety, process control in all the links of the chain is becoming increasingly important.

INGREDIENTS

Finished products typically consist of several ingredients. Should something be wrong with one of these ingredients, chances are great that this fault is also observed in the finished product. That is why it is of the utmost importance to carry out a stringent check on all incoming ingredients, for freshness and bacteriological quality. This inspection can be split into a visual and flavour check. The visual inspection will check for use-by date, certificates, undamaged packaging and mentions on the label. It will also confirm whether it actually involves the requested product. During the flavour inspection we check physical properties such as texture, hardness, delicacy and potential deviating flavours (e.g., by checking for

rancidity and oxidation in cream, milk, butter, nuts and fats).

STORAGE

The majority of ingredients are best protected against light and air and must be kept in a cool and odourless environment where the relative humidity does not exceed 70%. Strong-smelling products should not be stored in the same space. Raw materials and finished products should also be stored separately.

PRODUCTION

Typically the production space must be constructed and laid out in such a way that there is no risk of contamination (bacterial or other), which may lead to flavour deviations. For example, we have to keep wood out of the workshop, since wood is porous and hence highly contaminating. We also avoid all manner of odour sources (e.g., drainage pipes, smoking, perfumes, etc.), variations in temperature and too much light incidence.

PACKAGING

The cocoa butter in chocolate rapidly absorbs environmental odours when exposed to air. It is therefore of the utmost importance that the finished products be packaged as quickly as possible. The proper packaging will protect the products against light, moisture, loss of aroma, absorption of odours and damage. Improper packaging may be responsible for an unacceptable flavour in the finished product. For example,

PACKAGING MATERIAL TO BE AVOIDED	MATERIAL LESS LIKELY TO LEAD TO FLAVOUR DEVIATIONS
• Polystyrene foam • Cardboard • Wood shavings	• Polypropylene • Polyethylene • Tin

cardboard and plastic flavour, wood and printing ink can result in the product no longer complying with its quality requirements.
Not only do the barrier-like properties play a role, but the quality of the material's density and the sealing of the packaging are also of importance. The sealing must be of such a type that the packaging does not lose any of its properties. The choice of sealing – such as glue – may be a source of flavour contamination. The use of suitable packaging material and proper storage is a must.

STORAGE

The products must be stored at a specific distance from the floor and the walls, for example on plastic pallets or on metal racks. Finished products must be stored separately from ingredients. After each use we must carefully repackage and seal the remaining ingredients. We should label them with contents and dates. Packaging material must also be stored in a separate space.

TRANSPORT

As producers we must ensure that the same storage conditions are provided during transport and storage.

CONSUMERS

A factor not to be underestimated is what happens to the finished products when they end up in the shops. On the one hand it is important that shop assistants offer the products undamaged under appropriate preservation conditions, on the other hand, consumers must be made aware of how to best preserve the product for consumption.

CONCLUSION

It is important to take into account all factors from development on, with respect to production, storage, transport and correct information provided by the seller to the consumer. The road to acquiring a good reputation and notoriety is long and difficult, the road to losing your reputation is quick and easy!

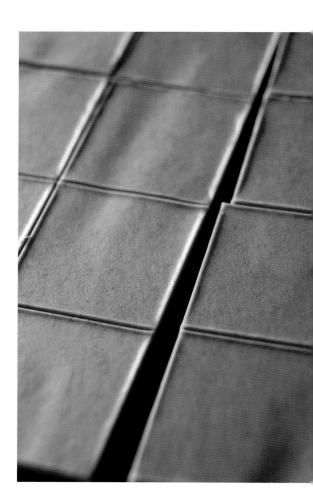

TRENDS IN THE CHOCOLATE WORLD

A trend is a direction in which something develops, something contemporary, something trendy. In order to develop a trend, it is important to push aside all (fear) barriers, which enables just anyone to be a trendsetter and which is more productive than being a trend follower. No idea is too crazy to try out, yet we must continue to think with the customer in mind, since after all, customers decide whether the product will be successful. For example, in the past 20 years we have seen massive shifts in trends.

Chocolate and its related products, such as praline and gianduja, were originally only used in confectionery and patisserie, but currently also pop up in the catering industry. The concept that these products processed in sauces and combined with fish, meat or cheese would be inedible, appeared to be false.

And all manner of exotic fruits from faraway places, such as passion fruit, papaya, mango, guava, kalamansi and lychee, made their appearance in the chocolate world. Then came the 'light' trend. Suddenly everything was too sweet, too fat and too high in calories. Consumers became increasingly aware of the impact of diet on their health. This increased scientific knowledge furthermore provided better insight into the options to create products capitalising on this concept.

Subsequently came the message that 'real' chocolate had to be dark, and not just dark, it was better if it made your hair stand on end, since only then was it true chocolate! The percentages of cocoa mass were increased to the extreme (99% cocoa mass and only 1% sugar).

Several chocolate producers then marketed 'origin chocolates'. And in order to continue to remain trendy at all costs, subsequently 'plantation'[1] and other exclusive chocolates were created.

An increasing number of spices found their way to the fillings; the more obscure and exclusive, the better!

Cream, butter and milk were no longer exclusively used for ganaches, but also all manner of teas, coffees, wines and beers. Especially the use of specialty beers, such as abbey and fruit beers, became popular – and they are currently abundantly processed in chocolate.

To put it briefly, the trends follow each other at an increasing pace. Whether all these trends will also be 'keepers', will obviously depend on consumers. Frequently resistance to change is significant among the latter. Therefore do not get discouraged too quickly when looking for something new.

A trend that nonetheless has been 'in' for quite some time and still is among professionals, is the creation of long-life pralines.

---

1   Plantation: Chocolate producers conclude an annual contract with local planters to exclusively purchase their entire annual yield.

Ingredients

ABOUT SUGARS AND FATS

Due to affluence in the Western world a lifestyle was created whereby consumers often take in more energy (in the form of fats and sugars) than necessary, which has a negative impact on body weight. Consuming less fat and less sugar is required in order to stay healthy. Fortunately there has been a clear evolution in the last decades in consumption behaviour in this area. The realisation that (over)consumption of fats and sugars is harmful to our health is clearly on the increase.

People also are increasingly aware that chocolate products are high in calories, fats and are very sweet. The use of fats and sugars is slowly decreasing and people think twice before being seduced by desserts and confectionery in general, which is a positive development.

It is therefore useful for chocolatiers to have a certain basic knowledge when using fats and sugars, resulting in them making fewer 'unintentional' errors in recipes and processing methods. And create loyalty among their customers. Other health aspects may also be of some importance in the chocolate sector and also require the necessary knowledge. For example, did you know that acrylamides (carcinogenic molecules) are created at high temperatures by bonding amino acids and sugars? And that transfatty acids have a significant negative impact on health (more particularly as regards cardio-vascular disease)?

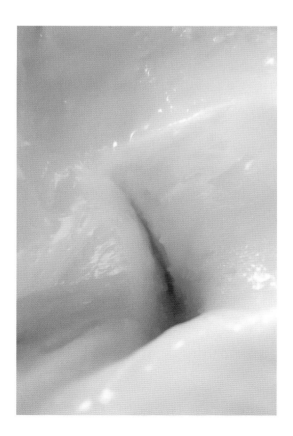

SUGARS

Traditionally sugar is the best liked sweetener and has developed into one of the major sources of carbohydrates in our daily eating patterns. These days conscious consumers are increasingly searching for healthy foods – with less sugar. In addition, both consumers and chocolatiers want pralines to have a longer shelf life.

Bulk purchases, which lower the prices, modern machines producing larger volumes and expensive wages, result in the majority of foodstuff requiring a longer shelf life. The contradiction in this context is that sugar in general contributes greatly to the shelf life of creams in chocolate items. Therefore professionals are practically forced to work with sugars.

Fortunately from a chemical point of view, there are a whole series of sugars, each with their specific properties and degrees of sweetness. Their energy will stay about the same.

Below is an overview of the major sugars and sweeteners.

Sucrose (or regular sugar), just like many other carbohydrates, is a major supplier of energy for our body. The energy content is approximately one quarter that of fats. In the digestion of sucrose, first the bond between the two units (a glucose unit and a fructose unit) must be broken up, resulting in the *availability* of the energy compared to glucose being slightly slower; yet sucrose is used in sports drinks, since the release of the units takes place quite rapidly, so that after consumption of an amount of sucrose a clear peak in blood sugar level can be observed.

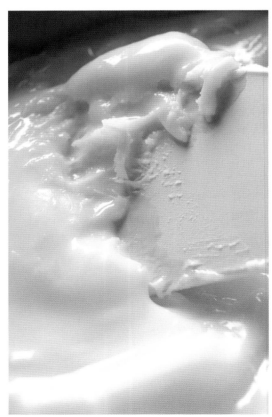

Schematic presentation of carbohydrates

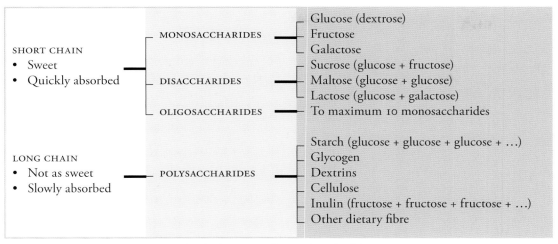

All carbohydrates are digestible and provide 4 kcal/g. Dietary fibre, inulin and cellulose are exceptions.

Extensive sweeteners

This group has a sweetening power on the same order as sucrose (equal to or less than sucrose) and does deliver energy. Extensive sweeteners are also referred to as bulking agents and include sugars, sugar alcohols (polyols), oligosaccharides and a number of polysaccharides.

In addition to sucrose it involves primarily glucose, invert sugar (a fructose-glucose mixture), maltose, lactose and fructose. Other sugars, such as maltulose, isomaltulose, lactulose and sugar alcohols such as sorbitol, xylitol, isomalt, maltitol, mannitol, isomaltitol and lactitol are also used.

Polyols naturally occur in various fruits and vegetables, but are also produced industrially.

NAME	AVERAGE RELATIVE SWEETNESS	STRUCTURE	PROPERTY
Sucrose	100	Disaccharide	
Lactose	40	Disaccharide (milk sugar)	
Maltose	50	Disaccharide	Malt aroma
Galactose	60	Monosaccharide	
Dextrose	70		Cold effect
Lycasin	70		Slightly bitter
Maltitol	90	Sugar alcohol (polyol)	Cold effect
Lactitol	40	Sugar alcohol (polyol)	Cold effect
Sorbitol	50	Sugar alcohol (polyol)	Cold effect
Isomalt	50	Sugar alcohol (polyol)	
Mannitol	70	Sugar alcohol (polyol)	
Xylitol	100	Sugar alcohol (Polyol)	Cold effect
Polydextrose	0	Polysaccharide	Slightly acidulous
Glucose syrup	74	In accordance with DE (= grape sugar)	
Glycerol	60		
Inulin	not available		
Oligofructose	30		

Relative sweetness (or sweetening strength) cannot be measured with an instrument. We draw comparisons by tasting and through flavour tests. As a result we find average values in the literature. In glucose syrups for that matter we will find highly divergent values since glucose syrup is always a mixture of various sugars. That is why, in glucose syrups, the DE value is initially a good measure for its sweetening strength.

Sucrose (white or household sugar)

Sucrose is a disaccharide, consisting of a glucose unit and a fructose unit (fruit sugar). This sugar has a strong sweetening strength and is probably still the most frequently used sugar. The degree of sweetness of sucrose is a point of reference and was established at 100. It is produced from sugar beets, sugar cane or sugar palm by means of a refining process in which the sugar from the plant is dissolved in hot water, and purified through filtration and recrystallisation. Chemically sugar is highly stable when surrounded by fat. It does not react with the fat. It can be bacteriologically contaminated, but the bacteria cannot develop due to the absence of water.

In fat phase fillings, the sugar particles surrounded by fat will dissolve in the mouth in proportion to the dimensions of the sugar. The released sweetness is part of the pleasant mouthfeel.

Sucrose is often used to extend shelf life and lowers the Aw value. Since it is a very inexpensive ingredient, it is used generously in water-based products in order to lower the finished product's cost price. Too high a dose in ganaches, however, may lead to early and undesirable crystal formation, typically resulting in rapid drying out.

It is also important to know that during the cooking process of a sugar solution, the sucrose is partially converted into invert sugar, which is for the most part beneficial for creams and ganaches, since invert sugar has the property to retain moisture resulting in the product not drying out as quickly. For hard confectionery, on the other hand, this is totally undesirable. Here the sugar solution must be cooked as quickly as possible until the desired temperature is reached.

Sucrose does not dissolve in alcohol. It crystallises (granulates) when oversaturated. Sucrose is also highly soluble: up to 2000 g sucrose can dissolve in 1000 ml water at room temperature. Around the boiling point this can even reach 5000 g.

Sucrose is chemically converted and starts to caramelise at 168°C (334°F). Caramelised sucrose provides aroma and colour.

Castor sugar

If it involves the brown version, we also refer to it as brown sugar or raw cane sugar. The process differs from manufacturer to manufacturer and from country to country. The basis is sucrose with impurities. The sap of the sugar cane or sugar beet is reduced, crystallised and strained. In order to obtain cassonade, treacle or caramel and in some cases, invert sugar, is subsequently added to the sugar. Castor sugar comes in white, yellow (light brown) and brown. The caramel gives the castor sugar slightly more flavour and a brown colour. Castor sugar contains more traces of water than granulated sugar. The darker the colour, the higher the moisture content. As a result of high moisture content this type of sugar becomes lumpy quite easily.

Isomalt

Isomalt is a polyol created by the hydrogenation of isomaltulose, which in turn is obtained through enzymatic transformation from sucrose. It is an odourless white crystalline powder. Isomalt is unusual since it is a synthetic polyol, produced from regular sugar. As an alternative natural sweetener it has a sweetening strength of 50 to 60 compared to sucrose. That is why it is often used as a bulking agent. Isomalt is heat- and pH-stable. It has a slight mouth-cooling effect and leaves no aftertaste. It enhances the flavour in other sweeteners and sugar alcohols, thus masking the bitter aftertaste of some other liquids. Due to its low hygroscopicity it is a well-liked product used to create sugar show pieces. It is also used in confectionery and bakery products.

Glucose

Glucose syrup is made through the hydrolysis (a breakdown process) of starch. Maize, wheat as well as potato starch are used. Depending on production conditions the conversion may be more or less intensive, which is decisive for the sweetening strength and viscosity. The degree of breakdown (polymerisation degree[2]) is expressed in DE[3] (dextrose equivalent). For example 53 DE will undergo stronger treatment than 46 DE. In nature glucose is created by plants during photosynthesis and further processed into starch for storage, among others.

The most frequently used ones are: 80% and 85% dry matter. Sweetening strength:
- glucose 60 DE (= 65),
- glucose 38 DE (= 45),
- glucose 30 DE (= 30).

---

2   Polymerisation is the bonding of small hydrocarbons into a long chain.

3   Dextrose equivalent is in fact the measure for the breakdown and is the opposite of polymerisation.

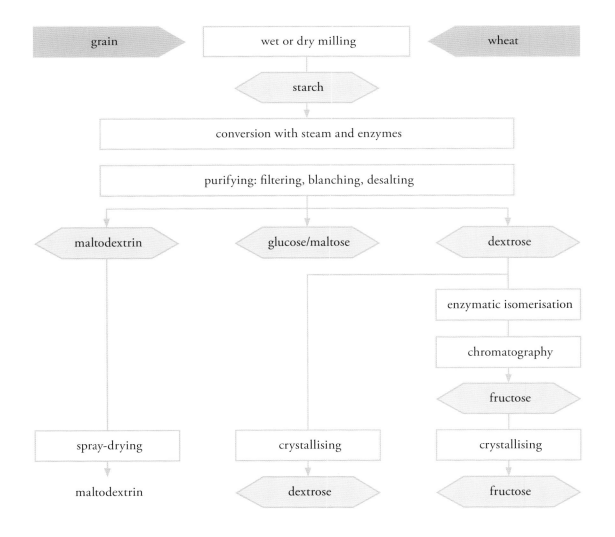

Glucose works hygroscopically (especially with high DE values). Low DE glucose increases viscosity, thickens slightly and strengthens (e.g., thin ganache structure).

Glucose with a low DE (< 40%) contains few reduced sugars, but many higher sugars and is recommended for hard drops, caramels, nougat, etc., since this quality is not highly hygroscopic, prevents deformation in a cold environment and counters the granulation of the sucrose.

Glucose with a high DE (> 45%) is primarily used for items containing a lot of water, such as marshmallows, since in this case the water-bonding properties of the reducing sugars slow down the drying out process.

Glucose limits and slows down crystallisation and lowers the Aw value. Due to the Maillard reaction, heated glucose provides aroma and colour.

Dextrose (grape sugar)

In its natural form D-glucose is referred to as dextrose or grape sugar. Its sweetening strength is 30, ideal for decreasing the sweetness in centres. It is relatively difficult to dissolve, decreases the average crystal size of the added sugars and provides certain flexibility, which can be useful in preparations such as fondant sugar. It has a 'cooling' effect in the mouth (only monohydrate), lowers the Aw value and is highly hygroscopic.

Polydextrose

Polydextrose is a bonded glucose polymer containing small quantities of sorbitol and citric acid. It is produced industrially, on the basis of sugar. It is a non- or low-sweetening, neutral, water-soluble polysaccharide. As a result it is often used as a bulking agent, and sugar or fat replacement. It is stable when used in a pH environment of 3 to 6.5. It has no cooling effect and is low in calories (1 kcal/g) since it is a dietary fibre. In this sense it is an appealing product for the production of low-calorie finished products. It is a tooth-friendly component and is also suitable for diabetics.

Dextrin

Dextrins are a group of carbohydrates with a limited number of glucose molecules in the chain, obtained through the hydrolysis of starch, whereby with the help of an acid and/or enzyme, the ingredient is partially broken down. They are shortened polysaccharides. Full hydrolysis results in the breakdown into glucose. Dextrins are powders that are fully or partially soluble in water. Since dextrins are harder to digest, they are sometimes added to foodstuffs to replace natural fibre. Other types of dextrin include maltodextrin, amylodextrin and cyclodextrin.

Maltodextrin

Maltodextrin is a high-quality carbohydrate made from potato, maize or grain starch through enzymatic hydrolysis. It is slightly sweet to tasteless and is primarily used as a fat imitator in pudding powders, sports drinks and coffee milk powders, to which it gives a slight gel-like structure. It is also a cheap additive, which decreases the sweetness in sweet recipes. It is a white hygroscopic spray-dried powder and is just as easy to digest as glucose.

Fructose (levulose)

Fructose (also referred to as fruit sugar) is a simple sugar. It is a white solid that is easily soluble in water. Honey, berries, melons and a number of tuberous plants contain large quantities of fructose. Industrially, it is primarily produced through separation, followed by the crystallisation of fructose from invert sugar syrups. Its sweetening strength is 130. It is able to prevent crystallisation and enhances the fruit aroma in fruit-containing filings. If fruit flavour is added, fructose also enhances the fruit flavour. It considerably decreases the Aw value, is highly hygroscopic and sensitive to temperature (caramel).

High-fructose syrups

Are created as a result of the breakdown of starch into glucose syrups and further (enzymatic) conversion of the glucose into fructose. The fructose content varies from 5% to 80% in dry matter, with concentrations of 70% to 80% in sugars. These syrups are highly hygroscopic and their functionality is comparable to invert sugar.

Invert sugar

Invert sugar contains approximately 50% dextrose and 50% fructose (in dry matter). It varies from semi-liquid to thick and syrupy, almost like semi-crystallised honey. It is marketed in concentrations of 70%, 75% and 80%. Invert sugar is obtained by heating sucrose under the influence of an acid, and subsequently neutralising the remaining acid with a base. Inversion can also be obtained by splitting regular sugar syrup with the enzyme invertase. This invert sugar has a better consistency and colour, but the inversion takes much longer (up to 7 days). Its sweetening strength is greater than that of sucrose (125). Since invert sugar is difficult to find in some countries, it is often replaced by honey, which in terms of composition is more or less the same. However, honey also contains vitamins, microorganisms and other substances (see below under honey). Invert sugar is able to prevent crystallisation, lower Aw value and has a hygroscopic effect. It is a desirable ingredient in items with high water content, which have to remain soft when stored. An excess of invert sugar, however, may lead to stickiness and syrup secretion. Typically up to 25% will yield a good result. When invert sugar is heated, it provides aroma and colour.

Invertase

Invertase is an enzyme used to invert sucrose into creams and syrups. Invertase is extracted from baker's or brewer's yeast. This enzyme is able to split sucrose into its two components, i.e., the simple reducing sugars glucose and fructose (= invert sugar). It is sold under various brand names and is marketed in a glycerol or sorbitol solution. The use of invertase is fairly limited due to its cost price and is often replaced by another enzyme converting glucose into fructose.

It is primarily used to make specific fillings softer by inverting the sugar. Most of the inversion takes place within 7 days (alcohol can curb the effect). The quantity varies between 2 to 5 g per 1000 g and is best added between 60 and 70°C (140-158°F). The pH must be contained between 3.8 and 5.2. If the temperature exceeds 70°C (158°F), the invertase activity is destroyed. A high acid content has the same effect on this enzyme. Invertase decreases viscosity. Its inverting action contributes to shelf life (by lowering the Aw value). It must be kept in a cool and dark place. Its use is regulated in a number of countries.

Honey

Honey is a natural sweetener produced by honey bees, with the nectar they gathered as the main ingredient. Nectar comes from flowers and contains several sugars, minerals and trace elements. Bees convert the nectar into honey by adding enzymes (diastase, invertase and catalase) and allowing the excess moisture in the nectar to evaporate.

Its composition differs depending on the plant variety and origin, but on average consists of:
- 18% water
- 38% fruit sugar (fructose): invert sugars
- 31% grape sugar (glucose): invert sugars
- 10% polysaccharides, minerals (especially manganese, iron, phosphorus and copper), organic acids (especially free amino acids) and vitamins
- 3% enzymes (or yeasts), hormones, gluconic acid, colouring and flavouring agents

Honey imparts a typical flavour to a product. Since honey contains microorganisms, it may be sensitive to fermentation in specific fillings. From a technical point of view remarks about invert sugar also apply here.

Lactose

Lactose (also referred to as milk sugar) is a natural sugar from the milk of all mammals, and from a few tropical plants. It is a disaccharide of galactose and glucose. Lactose is primarily extracted from whey through crystallisation or precipitation. Lactose is non-hygroscopic at stable temperatures up to 100°C. Its sweetening strength is 27. Lactose finely crystallises into sharp and hard crystals that are difficult to dissolve. The latter is especially important in the ice cream industry. Lactose lowers the Aw value and settles the aromas.

Tagatose

Tagatose is a bulk sweetener that does not belong to the polyols and appears as a natural sugar in fruit (apples, pineapple, etc.). It can also appear to a very limited degree in heat-treated dairy products. Its sweetening strength is 92% of regular sugar. This monosaccharide has practically no impact on the blood sugar level and is therefore suitable for diabetics. Tagatose is made from lactose (milk sugar) through a chemical process. Its flavour is neutral, like regular sugar. Even as a separate sugar replacement it behaves just like regular granulated sugar. Tagatose has a high melting temperature (134°C) and is stable with a pH from 3 to 7. Because it is a reducing sugar, it contributes more to browning reactions than sucrose (which is not reducing). Tagatose is only absorbed to a limited degree and as a result, it has a calorie contents that is lower than other sugars, i.e., 1.5 kcal/g.

Maltose (malt sugar)

Maltose is a disaccharide, made up of two monosaccharides of glucose. This type of sugar is created at the same time as dextrin when germinating grain due to the action of the existing diastase. It is relatively soluble at room temperature and solubility increases rapidly when the temperature rises. At approximately 90°C (194°F) solubility is equal to that of sucrose. Maltose occurs in high doses in glucose and malt extract. It is difficult to acquire for traditional chocolatiers.

Malt extract

Malt extract is primarily prepared from barley, sometimes also from other grains, and is a evaporated malt indication. It is used worldwide in the food industry as a flavouring agent. It consists of approximately 88% dry matter, and its average composition is:
- Moisture 22%
- Sucrose 4%
- Maltose 55%
- Dextrose and fructose 2%

- Dextrins 13%
- Proteins 3%
- Minerals 1%

Small doses are tolerated, yet must be listed on the packaging in compliance with European Union regulations.

Sugar alcohols or polyols

The name sugar alcohol is a chemical definition, it contains no alcohol (ethanol).

Sorbitol

Sorbitol is a natural sugar alcohol (polyol). It appears in various fruits such as apples, prunes, cherries and grapes but also in seaweed. It is primarily prepared industrially through the hydrolysis of starch or sugar. Sorbitol is available in powder form (E420i) and in a solution (E420ii). Sorbitol in powder form can come in four crystal forms, of which the melting points vary. The powder still contains approximately 1% water and must be stored in sealed packaging since it attracts moisture. It melts at around 110°C (230°F). Sorbitol in syrup form contains 30% water.

It is a limited moisture stabiliser, which inhibits the drying out of creams and ganaches, and lowers the Aw value. On the tongue it has a slightly cooling effect. It is a low-energy sweetener, has a relative sweetening strength (between 50 and 60), and is therefore highly suitable to replace part of the sugar in high sugar concentrations. The typical quantity is between 5 to 10%. If the quantity exceeds 5%, it is best to remove an equal quantity of glucose from the recipe in order not to affect the cream's texture. Sorbitol is sold under various brand names, which for the most part start with 'sor', e.g., Sorbex, Sorbit and Sorbo.

It is frequently used as a sweetener in light products, sugar-free diets, chewing gum and pastries. It prevents crystallisation. The acceptable daily intake (ADI) has no limit, but in excess of approximately 25 g per day, it becomes a laxative. With normal use and in normal applications, no side effects are to be expected, yet usage is limited in a number of countries. Sorbitol is highly stable against acids, enzymes and temperatures up to

140°C (248°F), but between 150-170°C (302-338°F) discoloration takes place. Sorbitol can be used in all religions, by vegetarians and by vegans.

Glycerol (glycerine)

Glycerol (E422) is also a sugar alcohol and is obtained through the hydrolysis of vegetable or animal fat or oil. It is a colourless, odourless and slightly sweet flavoured liquid with high viscosity. This smooth spreadable liquid gives creams and ganaches an unctuous and smooth feeling. Its relative sweetness (60) depends on the concentration. Glycerol is typically used as a stabiliser, thickener and wetting agent. It significantly lowers the Aw value and does not crystallise. It can be applied as liquid sorbitol. The typical quantity is around 3% and – just as in all polyols – becomes a laxative in high doses. A quantity above 12% furthermore results in a bitter burning flavour.

Mannitol

Mannitol is a polyol found in all manner of plant varieties, but especially in seaweed. It has a soft, cooling, sweet flavour and no aftertaste. The substance is non-hygroscopic and its sweetening strength lies between 60 and 70. Mannitol is used as a natural sweetener, anti-clumping agent and filler. It provides 1.6 kcal/g. It is prepared by catalytic hydrogenation of a mixture of glucose and fructose, prepared from invert sugar. Mannitol can also be produced by means of batch fermentation under aerobic conditions with the help of conventional strains of the yeast *zygosacharomyces rouxii*.

Mannitol can become a laxative with excessive use (average more than 15 g per day).

Since it has a high melting point (165-169°C), it is often used in ice cream. Mannitol is highly stable when heated and does not discolour at high temperatures.

Mannitol is also sometimes added since it provides an improved structure to specific foods and helps to stop them drying out.

Maltitol

Maltitol is prepared from the hydrogenation of maltose (starch). In an incomplete division, the glucose syrup also contains maltose. Maltose is a disaccharide consisting of two glucose molecules. If the glucose syrup is hydrogenated, the existing glucose is converted into sorbitol and the maltose partially into maltitol, thus obtaining maltitol syrup.

The sweetening strength of maltitol (90) is slightly lower than that of sugar. The energy value lies between 2 and 3 kcal per gram. Maltitol is hygroscopic and heat-resistant. There is no ADI.

Maltitol is used frequently in confectionery since it does not promote tooth decay.

Erythritol

Erythritol provides 0.2 kcal per gram and its sweetening strength is 60 to 80% compared to that of sucrose. The substance originates from an extract of fermented maize and/or wheat sugar. Erythritol is water soluble and melts at around 120°C. There is no ADI, but due to its laxative effect, the limit is 35 g per day. Erythritol is applied in confectionery, chocolate, light soft drinks, chewing gum, fillings, gelatine, jam and bakery products.

Xylitol

Xylitol can be naturally found in small quantities (< 1%) in fruit and vegetables. It is produced industrially through the hydrogenation of xylose. Its sweetening strength is approximately the same as that of sugar. Xylitol practically has the same properties as sugar and provides 2.4 kcal per gram. The sweetener is water soluble. The dissolving of xylitol in water is an endothermic process, whereby heat is removed from the environment, creating a fresh feeling in the mouth.

Xylitol is exclusively available for industrial purposes. It is processed in sugar-free chewing gum, etc.

Lactitol

Lactitol is a polyol and is produced from lactose or milk sugar, obtained from whey. Lactitol provides 2.4 kcal per gram and is nearly half as sweet as sugar. The sugar alcohol is water-soluble and heat resistant. When making pastries, lactitol is able to completely replace the sugar quantity. Lactitol does not cause tooth decay.

It is exclusively available for industrial applications, among which chewing gum. It is used as an artificial sweetener and as a laxative.

High-intensity sweeteners

High-intensity sweeteners are sweeteners of which the sweetening power is many times that of sucrose. Therefore the quantities that must be added to approximate the same sweetening strength, are much smaller than when sucrose is used. They do not lead to lower water activity. High-intensity sweeteners provide little to no energy and are consequently also often referred to as energy-free sweeteners.

Most high-intensity sweeteners, but also polyols, work in synergy, i.e., the sweetening strength of a mixture of sweeteners is greater than the sum of the individual sweeteners from said mixture. Furthermore mixtures of sweeteners often feature an improved flavour profile.

Although protein-based sweeteners can take part in Maillard reactions, high-intensity sweeteners seldom cause browning since the used concentrations are too low.

A number of high-intensity sweeteners were in fact brought up for discussion by scientists and legislators in connection with their potential carcinogenic nature under regular consumption.

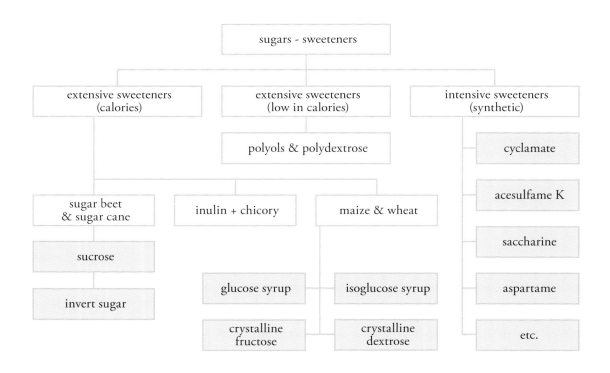

The following belong to the group of high-intensity sweeteners: aspartame, acesulfame K, cyclamate, saccharine and thaumatin, stevioside, glycyrrhizin acid, neotame, alitame, sucralose and neohesperidin.

Aspartame

From a chemical point of view, aspartame is a combination of two regular amino acids, asparagine acid and phenylalanine, with a methanol group in the phenylalanine portion. Aspartame provides 4 kcal per gram of energy, but little is needed and therefore no major energy input is provided when it is used. The ADI is established at 40 mg/kg of body weight per day. The sweetening strength of aspartame is 100 to 200 greater than that of sugar. Above 180°C the sweetener loses its sweetening power and is therefore not suitable for hot oven dishes, but can be added at the last moment to warm and hot dishes. Loss of sweetening strength may also occur if acid products (e.g., vinegar) are added. Aspartame resists freezing.

Aspartame is often used in combination with acesulfame K and is primarily applied in light products such as light soft drinks, yogurt drinks and other sweets. It is also used in a large number of other products, among which sweets and sweeteners, soft drinks, pudding powder, creams and fillings for pastry, ice cream, medicines, jam and marmalade, fruit mousse and chewing gum. Some people are unable to break down aspartame in the body, resulting in specific symptoms; hence the warning on the packaging of products containing aspartame.

Acesulfame K

The sweetening strength of acesulfame K is 130 to 200 times greater than that of sugar. Acesulfame K is not absorbed by the body, and consequently it provides 0 kcal/g of energy. The acceptable daily intake (ADI) is established at 9 mg/kg of bodyweight per day. This sweetener is heat-resistant up to 200°C, can be frozen and dissolves well in water. When adding acid products, such as vinegar, loss of sweetening strength may occur. Used often in combination with aspartame and primarily processed in bakery products and light products (light soft drinks and yogurt drinks).

Cyclamate

The sweetening strength of cyclamate is 30 to 80 times greater than that of sugar. Cyclamate provides no energy, withstands freezing and heating and dissolves well in water. The ADI is established at 7 mg/kg of bodyweight per day. This sweetener is used primarily in confectionery and light products such as light soft drinks, yoghurt drinks and desserts. Cyclamate is often used in combination with saccharine.

Saccharine

Saccharine is approximately 400 to 500 sweeter than sugar, highly water soluble and resistant to heating and freezing. The addition of milligrams to a foodstuff would have the same effect as the addition of grams of sugar. The ADI was established at 2.5 mg/kg of body weight per day.

Saccharine provides no energy since it is rapidly absorbed by the body and is practically eliminated by the body unaltered through urine. Saccharine has no impact on the glucose concentration in the blood, which makes it highly suitable for diabetics. It also causes no tooth decay. Saccharine is often used in combination with cyclamate. This sweetener is especially applied in 'light' products. Examples are yoghurt drinks, soft drinks, jam, bakery goods and salad dressings.

Thaumatin

Thaumatin is a natural sweetener and consists of various proteins, with the two most important ones being Thaumatin I (thalin) and Thaumatin II.

Thaumatin is a sweet flavoured protein originating from the berries from a tropical African plant. There are likely to be a number of related proteins in this plant. Like any other protein, thaumatin provides 4 kcal per gram. Its sweetening strength depends on the various protein fractions, varying from 1600 to 3000 times that of sugar, with an average of 2500. This sweetener has a slowly working and persisting sweetness, which allows it to be used easily with other strong sweeteners. Thaumatin is resistant to heating and has a liquorice-like aftertaste. It is exclusively available for industrial applications. Examples include chewing gum and sweets. Its persistent sweet aftertaste is a major advantage, especially in chewing gum.

Stevioside (stevia)

The white crystalline powder extracted from the leaves of the subtropical stevia shrub, is called stevioside. Stevioside is a completely natural product that does not produce calories. Its sweetening strength is up to 300 times greater than that of sugar. The leaves of the plant are 45 times sweeter. The shrub is not toxic. Since it provides enormous sweetening strength, only small quantities have to be used. The leaves can be used in their natural state. Both the leaves and the pure stevioside extract can be cooked, since they are heat-resistant up to 200°C. In contrast with other non-caloric sweeteners it has no bitter aftertaste. The sweetener is non-fermentable and flavour-enhancing. Stevioside has all manner of applications, in soft drinks, pastries, fruit juices, sweets, jam, yoghurt, chewing gum, sorbets, etc. Its use, however, is only authorised in Japan and a number of other countries. It is banned in the EU; in the US and Canada use is only authorised in food supplements.

Glycyrrhizin acid

Glycyrrhizin acid is a natural sweetener produced from the root of the liquorice plant (*glycyrrhiza glabra* or liquorice). Its energy value is negligible. Compared to sugar, glycyrrhizin acid has 30 to 50 times more sweetening strength. This sweetener works more slowly, sticks in the mouth and has a typical (liquorice-like) flavour. This liquorice plant is native to the Mediterranean, Russia and China.

The liquorice root contains approximately 1 to 25% of the glycyrrhizin substance. The liquorice root extract is released when the roots are ground and rinsed with hot water, thus creating block liquorice, which is the most important ingredient for liquorice. Due to its liquorice-like flavour glycyrrhizin acid is primarily used as a flavour enhancer, especially in liquorice, sweets and specific drinks. It is also an important in-

gredient in ouzo, pastis, pernod, various Belgian beers, liquorice tea and various types of herbal teas. Lastly, it is also found in chewing gum, cough syrup, throat lozenges, tobacco and obviously also in liquorice.

Sucralose

Sucralose is a new high-intensity sweetener produced from regular sugar (sucrose) by means of controlled chlorination. Sucralose has no energy value. Its sweetening strength is 600 greater than that of sucrose, but it does taste the same as regular sugar. It does not have a bitter aftertaste, is stable at high temperatures and dissolves easily in water. Sucralose is used in pastries, grain products, soft drinks, chewing gum, processed fruit and desserts.

Neotame

Depending on its application, neotame is 7,000 to 13,000 sweeter than regular sugar.

It is a water-soluble, heat-stable, crystalline powder that can be used both as a table sweetener and in warm preparations in the kitchen.

Alitame

Alitame consists of aspartic acid, alanine and an amino. Compared to aspartame it is a much stronger sweetener. Its sweetening strength is approximately 2,000 greater than that of sucrose.

Dihydrochalcones

Dihydrochalcones are sweeteners derived from the bitter-tasting flavonol glycosides in the peel of various citrus fruits. Typical examples are naringin (in grapefruit – *citrus paradisi*), neohesperidin (in the bitter orange or Seville orange – *citrus aurantium*) and hesperidin (in the regular sweet (navel) orange – *citrus sinensis*).

By means of simple chemical conversions highly potent sweeteners are created from these bitter substances, with a sweetening strength 2,000 times greater than that of sugar. In addition, for the first

FAT IMITATORS

Fat imitators are physically, chemically, enzymatically altered polymers, which display fatty properties in a cream's water phase. Contrary to fat, they are 'soluble' in water. To a certain degree they replace the mouthfeel of fat, but are not always able to take over the other functions. Fat imitators typically provide less aroma than the fat they replace since they contain water-soluble and not fat-soluble aroma components. Should we still want to include fat-soluble aroma components, we must make use of emulsifiers.

The major carbohydrate -based imitators include: dextrin and maltodextrin, gums, inulin, polydextrose, cellulose and β-glucans (or beta-glucans).

Protein-based fat imitators can be created from various protein sources such as eggs, milk, whey, soya, gelatine and wheat gluten. Their functional property is primarily aimed at the change in mouthfeel since they more or less mimic the texture of fat. In addition, they can also help with the stabilising of emulsions in spreads, sauces and dressings.

Overview of a few fat imitators

Dextrin and maltodextrin
(see 'Sugars' on page 16)

Dextrin and maltodextrin are decomposition products of starch. They absorb water thus forming a gel structure, which imitates the texture and mouthfeel of fat.

Gums (see page 42)

Gums are soluble fibres. They can be used as a fat replacement to imitate the creamy mouthfeel of fat and as a stabiliser for emulsions.

Inulin

Inulin is obtained through extraction with warm water from the chicory root and is 100% natural. Even though inulin is a sugar, it does not have a sweet flavour. This white creamy substance is an ideal fat replacement and bulking agent. Inulin lowers calories and is considered to be a fibre. It is primarily used together with a sugar replacement and/or sweetener. Due to its longer chain, inulin is less soluble in cold water than oligofructose, creating a gel in a watery environment. This inulin gel consists of a three-dimensional network of insoluble fine particles and imitates the mouthfeel of fat.

Polydextrose (see 'Sugars' on page 16)

Polydextrose is a non- or barely sweetening, neutral, bulking and water-soluble polysaccharide. Due to its bulking property, polydextrose is able to absorb the loss of volume coupled with fat reduction.

Cellulose

Cellulose is the main constituent of plant cell walls. As regards the use of cellulose in food-stuffs, we must make the distinction between cellulose fibres and purified cellulose preparations and derivatives. Cellulose fibres are considered to be ingredients and may be freely used. Purified cellulose on the other hand, is considered to be an additive (E460), and hence its use is limited.

Protein sources

Eggs

Since eggshells are highly contaminated with respect to bacteria (salmonella), it is recommended to always use pasteurised eggs. The use of raw eggs is banned in many countries.

COMPOSITION

The most frequently used eggs are chicken eggs. An average chicken egg weighs approximately 66 grams. An egg consists of 60% egg white (with ovalbumin as its main component), of 30% egg yolk, and of 10% egg shell. The yolk represents a single cell. The colour of the yolk may vary from very light yellow to dark orange. The colour of the yolk is determined by carotene and depends on the chicken's feed. The egg shell is approximately 0.3 mm thick. On the shell's inside two thin membranes protect the egg white against bacterial contamination. The shell is porous and therefore breathable.

The nutritional value of an egg totals 80 kcal (334 kJ), provided by 7.3 g protein, 5.8 g fat and 0 g carbohydrates. Furthermore eggs contain a number of minerals – such as phosphorus, potassium, sodium, calcium and iron – and the vitamins A, B1, B2, B6, biotin and E.

Chicken egg whites consist of 90% water molecules and 10% egg white (protein) molecules. When heated the thus far entangled egg whites roll out into long threads and form a network that solidifies, in which the water is caught. Egg white solidifies at a temperature of 63°C, egg yolk at 68°C.

Dairy

CREAM

Cream has a fat content of 30 to 40%. In this book cream with 40% fat content is typically used in cream recipes. The average composition of 100 g of cream is: 57.71 g water, 2.05 g egg whites, 37 g butterfat and the remainder carbohydrates.

MILK POWDER

The two types of milk powder available on the market are roller-dried or spray-dried milk powder. The latter is preferred since it dissolves more

easily and is finer. Whole milk powder contains a maximum of 5% water, at least 25-30% fat and 70% fat-free dry milk components. Skimmed milk powder contains a maximum of 5% water and at least 95% fat-free dry milk components.

The average composition of whole milk powder per 100 g is: 2.47 g water, 26.32 g protein, 26.71 g butter fat, 6.08 g ash and 38.42 g carbohydrates (sugars).

The average composition of skimmed milk powder per 100 g is: 3.16 g water, 36.16 protein, 0.77 g butter fat, 7.93 ash and 51.98 carbohydrates (sugars).

BUTTER

Butter is an emulsion of fat in water. Butter contains at least 82% fat and a maximum of 16% water. The average composition in the grams is: 17.94 g water, 0.85 g protein, 81.11 butter fat, 0.04 g ash and 0.06 g carbohydrates (sugars).

RICE MILK

The average composition in grams is: 89.28 g water, 0.28 g protein, 0.97 g fat, 0.30 g ash, 9.17 g carbohydrates, 0.3 g fibres and 5.28 g total sugars.

SOYA BEANS

With a moisture content (primarily water) of the soya bean of 11%, the average percentages of the remaining components are: 18% oil (of which 0.5% lecithin), 37% protein, 28% carbohydrates and 6% raw fibre.

This composition makes soya a noble food, all the more so since the oil provides essential amino acids, fatty acids and the egg whites eight essential amino acids. From all vegetable proteins , the protein composition of soya is the only one to be 'complete', i.e., all eight essential amino acids are contained in it. Soya beans are also particularly rich in vitamins and minerals. The soya bean is rich in polyunsaturated fatty acids and contains no cholesterol. Soya beans are furthermore an excellent source of calcium, iron, zinc, phosphate, magnesium, vitamin B and folate.

EMULSIFIERS

Emulsions are mixtures of liquids that are not miscible. Emulsifiers ensure that the emulsion is more easily formed and/or will not curdle.

Lecithin

Lecithin is a fatty substance primarily produced from soya bean oil. In recent years lecithin is being increasingly extracted from other sources, such as sunflower seeds. Lecithin is also found in egg yolk and in vegetable rapeseed and maize

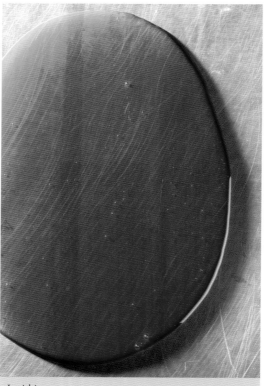

Lecithin

oils. Due to its fatty structure, lecithin easily dissolves in fat. The phosphoric acid group, however, easily dissolves in water. As a result fat can form an emulsion with water. In the chocolate industry lecithin is used to improve the fluid properties (both viscosity and yield point), since it better distributes the expensive cocoa butter. At temperatures above 60°C lecithin partially loses its effect.

Polyglycerol polyricinoleate (PGPR)

PGPR is an emulsifier, which significantly lowers the yield point in chocolate. It is produced artificially and is a combination of polyglycerol and fats from oil from the tropical castor oil plant (ricinus sp.). Typically fat consists of glycerol and fatty acids, but in this substance both the glycerol and the fatty acid from castor oil are polymerised, resulting in a highly complex product. PGPR has an E number (E476) and is authorised in chocolate up to a quantity of 0.05 to 0.2%. The difference between lecithin and PGPR is that lecithin lowers the viscosity of the chocolate and that PGPR lowers the yield point. During tempering PGPR keeps the chocolate fluid longer. PGPR in combination with lecithin provides better viscosity stability than lecithin alone, but this obviously also depends on the recipe. PGPR is also frequently applied in bakery products. Its use is approved in all religions and by vegetarians and vegans.

COLLOIDS

A colloid is a chemical mixture whereby a substance (colloid) is dispersed within another substance.

A colloidal system therefore consists of two separate phases: a dispersed phase and a continuous phase. A colloid system is solid, liquid or gaseous. The particles of the dispersed substance remain in suspension in the mixture. It is different from a solution in which the particles are dissolved. In a colloid mixture the particles are larger than in a solution. They are still small enough to be distributed in a liquid with a homogenous aspect, but also large enough to scatter light and not to dissolve it. That is why some colloid mixtures have the appearance of solutions.

The dispersed-phase particles have a diameter between approximately 5 and 200 nanometres. Such particles are invisible to an optical microscope.

When referring to a homogeneous mixture, we can state that the particles measure less than $10\text{-}9^m$. If between $10\text{-}9^m$ and $10\text{-}6^m$ we refer to colloid mixtures and in particles greater than $10\text{-}6^m$ non-homogeneous mixtures.

Some emulsifiers, stabilisers, thickening agents and gelling agents belong to colloid mixtures.

Emulsifiers

Emulsifiers are substances that keep the particles floating in an emulsion. They make it possible for two non-miscible phases to blend into a more or less stable product. Emulsifying therefore means dispersing a very fine substance in a liquid. Milk (fat-protein bubbles in water), butter (fat bubbles in water) and soya beans contain emulsifiers naturally. The most frequently used emulsifiers for the chocolatier are soya lecithin and PGPR (Polyglycerol Polyricinoleate).

Stabilisers

Are often added to lightly dissolving substances to extend shelf life or improve transportability. They therefore ensure that the mixture of two non-miscible substances is maintained.

Thickening agents

Thickening agents are ingredients that are able to bond water by creating a gel and thus thickening the final product. They consist for the most part of carbohydrates. The most frequently used thickening agents for solutions with high viscosity are gelatine, pectin, alginates, locust bean gum and guar gum. For solutions with slightly lower viscosity they are agar-agar and starch. And for solutions with low viscosity they are gum arabic and dextrin (hydrolysis of starch).

Gelling agents

Gelling agents are specific thickening agents. Under certain circumstances they form a reversible or non-reversible molecular network structure thus achieving extra firmness. They alter consistency and give products a gelatinous structure.

Gums

Gums are soluble fibres used to influence the viscosity of foodstuffs, and as stabilisers for emulsions. Small 2% concentrations can lead to gel and film formation as well as an increase in viscosity. Gums are sometimes used as fat replacements to imitate the creamy mouthfeel of fat.

TRAGACANTH GUM (E413)

Tragacanth gum is a white to whitish yellow, colourless powder and is used as a thickener, stabiliser and emulsifier. It is a natural polysaccharide and is produced from the dried slimy sap of some 20 plant varieties of the genus asteracantha in south-eastern Europe and south-western Asia. With low concentrations no side effects are known; with high concentrations, however, just like other non-digestible polysaccharides (nutritional fibre), it may cause flatulence and a bloated feeling due to the fermentation of the substance by the intestinal flora.

AGAR-AGAR (E406)

Agar-agar is an unbranched polysaccharide obtained from the cell walls of some species of algae. It is used as a gelling or binding agent, for the preparation of fruits, pudding and jam (jelly), among others. Chemically, agar-agar is a polymer, made up of subunits of galactose. Its binding power is two to four times greater than that of (animal) gelatine and makes it an ideal alternative for vegetarians.

The name comes from the Malay, where it is a term for the jelly-like mass from red algae. Agar-agar used to come mainly from Japan, where it is primarily used as a binding agent for soups, ice cream and desserts and flavoured and coloured jellies. Currently agar-agar is sourced in various, especially Asian, countries.

It is available in the form of slightly compressed strips, flakes, sticks and powder, and also in unrefined form (grey). Sticks and flakes require a cooking time of approximately 20 minutes. Powder only needs a few minutes. If it is overheated is may lose binding strength; when underheated it does not achieve its full binding strength. The sticks must first be thoroughly soaked in plenty of water and subsequently squeezed. In recipes with a low pH (e.g., specific fruits, specific origin chocolates) the bond strength is not as strong.

The soaked agar-agar is slowly heated in (a portion of) the required liquid under constant stirring until fully dissolved. This syrup can then, while still warm and liquid, be added to the dish, unless it involves a cold mass, containing whipped cream and/or egg whites. In the latter case we must first allow the agar-agar syrup to cool, until just barely liquid.

Syrup that is too cold and stiff can be made liquid again through heating. Since agar-agar rapidly stiffens when cooled, we always have to stir thoroughly before pouring the syrup into the mass, preferably using a whisk, but not for too long (a few seconds) and especially not using a hand mixer.

1 g agar-agar allows 1 dl watery liquid (juice, broth) to gel. Voor mixed liquids in which heavy cream, cottage cheese, milk or egg white is processed, a little more is required. 1 g of agar-agar replaces 3 g of gelatine. Agar-agar furthermore stiffens faster than gelatine and also remains stiff outside the refrigerator. In order to improve consistency we can combine agar-agar with arrowroot in some dishes.

GUM ARABIC (GUMMI ARABICUM)

Gum arabic is the hardened sap of the *acacia arabica*. It is a mixture of polysaccharides and glycoproteins, and is fully edible. It resembles a resinous gum, but it is no resin (resins do not dissolve in water, but in alcohol). Gum arabic slowly dissolves in water, and is slightly hygroscopic. In its pure form the gum is of a yellowish colour. The gum must be thoroughly cleaned since it is contaminated with impurities and bacteria.

Gum arabic is used as an additive in foodstuffs, namely as a thickener, emulsifier and stabiliser. Its applications are similar to gelatine, but gum arabic is also suitable for vegetarians. In the production of sweets, quite a lot of gum arabic is processed in gumdrops, i.e., between 35% and 45% of its composition.

WHIPPING AGENTS

We do not only make creams lighter and increase their volume for the flavour we experience, but also to keep down the cost price. Aeration can take place in two ways:

- When the cream to be aerated has enough ingredients to guarantee a certain stability after air input, we can increase the volume through mechanical air input, which requires special equipment.
- Another method is by folding a foamy mass into the cream. This mass, most often referred to as *frappé*, is foam on the basis of egg whites, soya proteins, dairy proteins and gelatine. Frappé must possess and more particularly be able to maintain the necessary stability once it is blended with the basic recipe. Obviously the quantity of frappé to be added depends on the degree of airiness we expect from the cream.

EGG ALBUMIN

Contributes to a major increase in volume. This foam is light, but brittle in texture. Egg albumin is sensitive to a low pH, thus limiting the storage of the proteins. The sensitive foam does not keep well, and is therefore not suitable for products requiring long shelf life. Egg albumin is furthermore quite expensive.

SOYA PROTEIN

Soya protein is one of the most heat-resistant whipping agents. This stability results in soya protein being more versatile than other whipping agents. Soya proteins work well with a broad range of pH values. It is nonetheless difficult to disguise the soya flavour.

MILK PROTEIN

Milk protein is a relatively stable whipping agent. We are, however, unable to whip it into a light foam as with other whipping agents; milk protein yields a firmer foam. Milk protein does have a typical flavour, which may or may not be desirable. Compared to other whipping agents it is also fairly expensive. Milk protein may also cause allergic reactions, which is why it is obligatory to always mention its use.

GELATINE

Gelatine is the most stable whipping agent. The foam obtained varies from soft to stiff.

Gelatine works well in nearly all pH environments and is valuable due to its versatility.

SHELF LIFE

Sometimes a long period elapses between a product's production and its consumption. Depending on the manufacturer, the product may be consumed after a few hours or after many months. It is clear that this period must be bridged by the product's shelf life. Below we will further discuss the physicochemical and microbial processes determining the shelf life of chocolate products.

Definition of shelf life

Shelf life is the period during which a product produced 'under normal circumstances' and relevant storage conditions, without unacceptable microbiological growth, chemical or flavour-related changes, is therefore suitable for sale and consumption, which implies that the product must initially be of high quality.

Even if produced under proper hygiene conditions and stored in the correct circumstances, a number of products undergo changes shortly after production, without, however, making the products unacceptable to consumers. The processes limiting the shelf life of chocolate products, can be classified into three categories:

- Microbial spoilage
- Chemical spoilage
- Physical spoilage

Often said processes occur in combination or as a result of each other.

Microbial spoilage

Microbial spoilage is obviously caused by microorganisms, which may be moulds, yeasts or bacteria. They may end up in the product through the ingredients, environment, machines or personnel.

Mould spores are present everywhere, both outdoors and indoors, but are especially prevalent in places where fresh food products are processed. All material and equipment must always be thoroughly cleaned, since microorganisms easily develop on them. Personnel can also be carriers. Entrepreneurs have a major responsibility for the (consequences) of the discovery of contamination.

Untreated foodstuffs or environments are never sterile. Germs are ubiquitous. That is why it is of the utmost importance to keep conditions so that the organisms present are unable to multiply and spoil the product. Depending on the type of or-

QUALITY

TIME

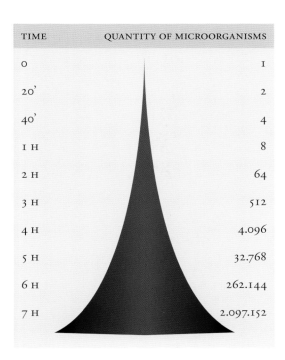

TIME	QUANTITY OF MICROORGANISMS
0	1
20'	2
40'	4
1 H	8
2 H	64
3 H	512
4 H	4.096
5 H	32.768
6 H	262.144
7 H	2.097.152

ganism, they require water and/or food stuffs (possibly also oxygen) to develop. Many microorganisms, however, do not require oxygen to develop. In order to avoid potential spoilage, mere airtight packaging is therefore absolutely not sufficient.

Temperature has a clear impact on the multiplication speed and activity of microorganisms. For further information see 'Shelf life' in *Fine Chocolates 1*, page 49-56 and *Fine Chocolates 2: Great Ganache Experience*, page 41).

To numerous microorganisms, 30 to 40°C is an ideal temperature. The temperature in the storage space, and especially the refrigerator temperature – slightly inhibit microorganisms, but only at deepfreeze temperature do all microbial processes stop. Microorganism spores, however, do not die off in the deep-freezer! Normal, proper storage conditions in terms of temperature for chocolate products vary between 10 and 20°C (50°F to 68°F), since they are easily achievable for practical, energy and cost reasons.

The following include a few examples of microbial spoilage:
- Fungus formation on the surface between filling and chocolate shell.
- Cracked pralines due to gas formation. Osmophilic yeasts convert sugars into CO_2 gas.
- Whipped cream fillings turning sour. Lactic acid converts sugars into organic acids. It is important to mention that this type of spoilage only makes the product unsavoury and certainly does not lead to medical complications.

Cracked pralines as a result of gas formation

Pathogenic microorganisms often barely affect the product's organoleptic quality, but do obviously pose a potential threat to consumer health.

Foodstuffs (sugars, proteins, fats, water, etc.) are abundantly present in chocolate products.

The quantity of available water is a very important factor in microbial spoilage and obviously highly dependent on moisture content, but also on the nature of the other ingredients.

The majority of ganache recipes contain a lot of water from the ingredients, since water gives the ganache its pleasant, creamy smooth and light structure. And it is in fact this water that represents the culture medium for numerous microorganisms such as fungi, yeasts and dangerous bacteria such as salmonella and listeria. As it happens, many ingredients, such as milk, cream, pure fruit juice or fruit pulp, primarily consist of water.

A recipe's total moisture content only provides limited information about shelf life. Shelf life actually depends on the quantity of water available to microorganisms and to chemical reactions. The water present can therefore be available to a greater or lesser degree, or just be bound. How much water is bound, depends on the further composition of the ganache. For example, water forms a strong bond with sugar or as crystallisation water.

Water activity

Water activity or Aw value for short, indicates how much water is available in a food product for all manner of reactions and is therefore a better measure for the risk of microbiological spoilage than the moisture content itself. Physically, Aw is the vapour pressure of water above a specific food product divided by that of pure water at the same temperature. The Aw value is an abstract number and is always greater than 0 and smaller than 1. Water activity depends on the temperature and increases with rising temperatures. Water activity in the fillings is measured at the temperature at which the filling is distributed and sold (for the most part around 20°C or 68°F). It is expressed on a scale from 0 to 1, where:

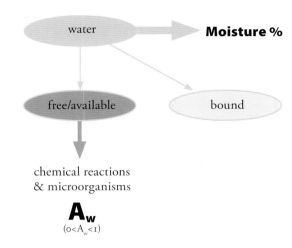

- 0 = complete dry mass or solid ingredients
- 1 stands for 100% water
- 0.5 stands for a solution corresponding to the activity of 50% free water

Calculation of the Aw value on the basis of composition is only possible by approximation, hence not sufficiently precise and as a result but only as an indication. It is nonetheless possible for simple sugar solutions, but due to the complexity of a ganache as a result of the various solubilities of the different sugars and other ingredients, it is not possible to accurately calculate an Aw value for it. Water activity can be measured by means of a fairly simple instrument, i.e., the Aw meter, which measures the relative humidity above the food product in a specific container. In other words, the humidity in the air is measured when it no longer extracts moisture from the product or vice versa. Hence in some trade literature reference is made to ERH (Equilibrium Relative Humidity[4]). With fillings containing alcohol, a faulty reading may occur. The purchase of an Aw meter is only warranted if used frequently.

4　Equilibrium Relative Humidity or ERH (balanced in relative humidity) is the point at which the product attracts no water from the environment and provides no water to the environment.
The ERH is expressed as a percentage, whilst the Aw is expressed as a decimal value, e.g., ERH 70% = 0.7 Aw.

PRALINE FILLINGS

To be distinguished:
* Water-based fillings
* Water/fat-based fillings
* Fat-based fillings

Water-based fillings

These fillings contain no fat. Typical examples include fruit pastes, fondant sugar fillings, marshmallows, liqueur fillings, etc.

Fruit pastes

Fruit pastes are mostly sold as separate products, but they also come as fillings for pralines, which are combinations of sugars and fruit pulp with a thickener. For further information and recipes see *Fine Chocolates 1* page 212.

Fondant sugar

Fondant sugar is a creamy sugar mass, consisting of a mixture of sugars and water, heated between 114°C (237°F) and 118°C (244°F). When cooled the mass changes into a supersaturated sugar syrup, which is subsequently processed to obtain a fine crystal structure. The addition of invertase to a filling may result in the filling becoming softer after processing and achieving a creamy texture. After addition of 0.4% invertase the filling may become softer after some two weeks. If the chocolate shows fine tears, the invertase increases the risk of leakage, which is why it is critical when pouring the moulds to agitate thoroughly to ensure that all air bubbles are removed from the chocolate. A properly shaped shell is

therefore of the utmost importance. For further information and recipes see *Fine Chocolates 1*, pages 77-78.

Fillings containing fruit dough, fondant sugar and marshmallow typically contain little moisture and therefore problems can be expected with respect to microbiological spoilage with microorganisms, which are able to survive at these low Aw values. For further information about Aw value see page 62.

So-called osmophilic yeasts and xerophilous moulds may cause problems in fillings with fruit pastes or fondant sugar. In particular fondant sugar fillings must be processed very hygienically in order to prevent contamination by these microorganisms. A typical example of contamination with osmophilic yeasts are pralines cracking (e.g., with fondant sugar fillings). Especially when stored at higher temperatures microorganisms multiply rapidly (see page 49).

Marshmallows

Marshmallows are highly sensitive to drying out and therefore are not really subject to microbiological spoilage.

Liqueur fillings

Examples of pralines with liqueur filling are cerisettes or cherry pralines and liqueur pralines with liquid filling. For further information and recipes see *Fine Chocolates 1*, page 178.

If at least 17% pure alcohol of the total free water + alcohol is processed in the recipe, we prevent all microbiological growth is prevented and there is no problem with bacteriological spoilage.

In high alcohol concentrations, and especially if there is direct contact between the alcohol and the chocolate shell, problems may arise with the chocolate shell, which will turn soft after a given storage time (depending on storage conditions). The alcohol migrates through the chocolate shell and evaporates and hence the filling will dry out, resulting in the implosion of the chocolate shell. That is why industrial liqueur pralines are made of chocolates without lecithin as they have a high cacao butter content, which makes the chocolate more resistant to the migration of alcohol and water.

With the use of liquid fillings in moulded pralines we must pay special attention when closing the chocolate shells, lest the filling blends with the chocolate during sealing, resulting in an unpolished finished product or leaking pralines. That is why it is recommended to allow the surface of the filling to first form a slight crust.

It is recommended to heat fondant cream fillings slowly before piping it into chocolate shells in order to speed up crystallisation and promote the crusting of the surface.

In addition, we must ensure that when filling the chocolate shells no filling particles end up on the edge of the shell, since this will inhibit full sealing, with leakage as a potential result.

Another reason for leakage may be the insufficient bonding of the bottom, since the shell chocolate is too crystallised. Therefore always slightly heat the shell edge, allowing the bottom to adhere to it.

Water/fat-based fillings

Water/fat-based fillings are emulsions. In an emulsion two non-miscible products are brought together, in this case water and fat. One of the two products is the continuous phase, in which the other phase is finely distributed in drops, as in ganache preparations.

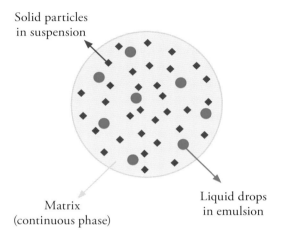

Solid particles in suspension

Matrix (continuous phase)

Liquid drops in emulsion

If we add cream to liquid chocolate, the chocolate will initially thicken, until the emulsion shifts, and the chocolate will thin if more cream is added. Initially there was water (water/oil) in fat emulsion, which subsequently changes into a fat in water emulsion (oil/water). Two non-miscible phases are mixed anyway and as a result, the system is in theory unstable; and the risk of separation is high, which is referred to as shifting.

Emulsifying ingredients

When a cold or tepid liquid (cooked and cooled) is added to melted chocolate, the chocolate initially thickens. The ganache is then in a melted fat phase in which water drops are emulsified. If more liquid is added, the mixture will become thinner again and suddenly also darker. The emulsion is now reversed, in other words, a water phase is now created in which the chocolate (fat phase) is emulsified. If we make sure that during this mixing, the temperature remains under 32°C (90°F), the mixture is tempered. The chocolate remains in the watery liquid in drop form.

58

- Minimum of 25% sugars:
  - Increases shelf life since they bond with water
  - Some sugars soften the structure
- For long shelf life a minimum of 75% dry substances in the total water quantity:
  - The more dry substances, the longer the product's shelf life

Extension of shelf life by adding alcohol

Shelf life can be considerably lengthened by adding pure alcohol. Alcohol is primarily effective against bacteria and slightly less against yeasts, but the majority of moulds are eliminated by adding 1% pure alcohol.

With 1% of the total water content in the recipe we already notice a slight difference, with 15% and up, we achieve high efficiency and with 17% the filling acquires an ideal shelf life – obviously provided that all storage conditions are satisfied. See 'Shelf life' on page 48.

Conversion formula to determine the required alcohol content

The calculation of the liqueur to be added to a recipe to achieve 17% added pure alcohol, is fairly laborious. Since not everyone is familiar with these formulas, a simpler method was developed to determine the correct quantity. This aid is referred to as the Pearson square, which is also frequently used by winemakers to adjust the degree of alcohol, acidity and sweetness. Using the Pearson square we are able to quite quickly and easily calculate the liqueur quantity needed to provide a ganache with the required amount of pure alcohol.

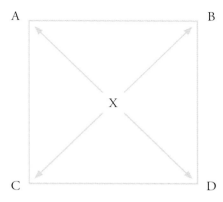

The four corners are A, B, C and D.
Firstly, we draw two diagonal lines and create the intersection X.
In corner A we put the total alcohol content in the filling's water phase (this is typically 0).
In C we put the alcohol content of the liqueur we wish to use.
X is the total alcohol content required for a bacteriologically non-perishable product (= 17%).
B is the difference between C and X.
D is the difference between X and A.
B : D = the ratio of the water phase B (parts B) to be mixed with the number (D) of parts of liquor.

EXAMPLE: CALCULATION OF AN 'EGG LIQUEUR' OR 'ADVOCAAT' RECIPE.

	WEIGHT IN WATER
90 g egg yolks	49% (= 0.49 x 90 = 44.1 g water)
350 g sweetened condensed milk	31% (= 0.31 x 350 = 108.5 g)
50 g glycerol	0 g
100 g maltodextrin	0 g
??? g liqueur 60%	
	TOTAL = 152 g water

ALCOHOL CONTENT

WATER PHASE = 0   (C-X = 43 PARTS WATER)

A ┌─────────────────────┐ B
  │   │
  │   │
  │   17   │
  │   (DESIRED   │
  │   ALCOHOL CONTENT) │
  │   │
  │   │
C └─────────────────────┘ D

60 (% ALCOHOL   (X-A = 17-0 = 17)
IN THE LIQUEUR)   = 17 PARTS LIQUEUR

If we have 43 parts (g) water, we have to add 17 parts liqueur.

For 1 part (g) we must therefore add 43 times less liqueur = 17 : 43 x 1 g.

But there is 152 g and therefore we must add 152 times 17/43: $\frac{152 \times 17}{43}$ = 60 liqueur to be added.

Same calculation but now written as a formula where A = 0:

$$XX = \frac{17 \, W}{(c-17)} =$$

W = weight of water in a non-liqueur ganache (e.g., 152 g)
C = alcohol% in liqueur (e.g., 60)
XX = unknown (gram liqueur to be added)

$$X = \frac{17 \times 152}{(60 - 17)} = 2584/43 = 60$$

II

Fat-based recipes

CHOCOLATE SPREADS

Definition of chocolate spreads or chocolate pastes: These are dispersions in which the reduced solid matter present in the discontinuous phase is distributed in the continuous phase, which could be an aqueous solution of sugars and possibly honey and/or milk ingredients. In this case, we refer to a water-based paste. If the continuous phase consists of fat, we refer to a fat-based paste. The continuous phase determines the properties of the paste.

The syrupy structure is typical of water-based pastes, which are very sweet, with rapid aroma release and fairly high energy value. The risk in water-based pastes is a potential structural breakdown due to bacteriological spoilage or granulation if the processing and/or recipe were not carried out correctly.

PROPERTIES OF WATER-BASED PASTES	PROPERTIES OF FAT-BASED PASTES
• more or less syrupy structure (whether bonded or not) • fast release of cocoa aromas • sweet • short structure • high energy value, depending on recipe	• soft structure • gradual release of cocoa/nut aromas • not as sweet as water-based pastes • higher energy value than water-based chocolate paste
RISKS	**RISKS**
• granulation of paste • microbiological growth	• separation of oil • oxidation of fats • recrystallisation of fats • difficult to spread (summer recipe < > winter recipe)

The unctuous structure is typical of fat-based pastes, which are less sweet with gradual aroma release. The problems that may occur in fat-based pastes if they are not properly formulated and/ or have undergone incorrect treatment, are the separation of oil in the paste, reaching insufficient spreadability in extreme ambient temperatures, formation of grains and fat oxidation.

Role of the most frequently used ingredients in water-based pastes

Cocoa ingredients

Fat-free cocoa ingredients are added as flavour and colour components. Alkalised powders may be used without technological objections, if desired for flavouring or colouring. Cocoa powder has an obvious impact on the paste's structure. In general an equal part of fat must be introduced for every part of cocoa powder left out in order to achieve an identical short structure.

Sugars

Sugars are used for their preserving action in addition to their sweetening strength. The limiting factor for use is solubility (max. 67% sugars at 20°C).

Invert sugar is often used together with sucrose in chocolate pastes. Glucose syrup may increase the sugar concentration thus enhancing the preserving action. Dextrose monohydrate clearly inhibits granulation. For other alternatives to sugars see 'Sugars' on page 16.

Fat

All oils and fats have a positive impact on structure and spreadability. Fat reduces the structure. When choosing the type of fat we have to pay attention to crystallisation speed, percentage of solid fat at room temperature as well as oxidation and flavour stability. Optimum spreadability is achieved with rapidly crystallising fats containing a considerable amount of liquid fat at room temperature. Given the aqueous environment, lauric fats are best avoided.

Milk ingredients

Have an obvious impact on flavour and structure, which will become stiffer and longer.

Emulsifiers

Several types of emulsifiers are available, which may have a certain impact on the structure of the paste. Many are nonetheless not authorised. Lecithin is the most frequently used emulsifier for this purpose.

Thickeners

Provide a more easily spreadable paste. The amount is minimal.

The processing of water-based pastes is relatively simple, and differs depending on the recipe used:
- Specific pastes are pasteurised at 85°C after the ingredients are mixed.
- Recipes with a high sugar/water content on the other hand, are heated to a specific temperature, depending on the ingredients used.
- Cooling must take place fairly rapidly.
- Filling takes place around 40°C and subsequently we must ensure rapid and full cooling before packaging the paste.

The impact of the most frequently used ingredients on fat-based pastes

Fat

This is the most important ingredient in this type of paste. Since fat constitutes the paste's continuous phase, it largely determines the properties of the finished product. In order to obtain a highly spreadable paste, in which oil will not separate and which does not shrink in the packaging, a fat system must be chosen in which small fat crystals retain the oil. There are two ways of achieving this:
- Fully liquid oil stabilised by a small percentage of a high-melting component. This method yields a paste with a high-gloss surface, spreadability between the oil's solidification point and the melting point of the solid component (very broad range), highly critical crystallisation behaviour and the required special cooling equipment.
- Fat mixture that contains sufficient solid matter at room temperature that stabilisation ensues. With this method the lustre is temperature-dependent. Spreadability depends, to a limited extent, on the percentage of solid matter in the fat mixture at the various temperatures. This method does not require special cooling equipment. These pastes have a higher viscosity structurally since the quantity of solid fat is greater than in a paste in the above-mentioned system. The use of polymorphic fats (cocoa butter) is to be avoided due to the risk of small fat crystal formation.

Nuts

Nuts are first and foremost intended to be flavour enhancers. The paste's flavour is determined by the choice of nuts and their roasting degree. In addition, nuts are important due to their oil content. Some nuts, such as walnuts, are highly sensitive to oxidation.

Cocoa powder

Non-alkalised powders are recommended for flavour reasons, preferably low-fat cocoa powders.

Milk ingredients

Low-fat milk powder is highly recommended, since it has a strong viscosity-increasing effect, thus preventing the separation of oil. If for flavour reasons, whole milk is chosen, it is recommended not to add more than 7% milk fat to the fat composition. That is why spray-dried powders are preferred over powders dried on cylinders. The limited use of whey powder and/or recombined whey products is sometimes desirable as they provide a darker paste, thus creating higher lustre.

Sugars

Practically the same rules apply here as to water-based pastes, with the exception of alternative crystalline sugars such as lactose or dextrose. Lactose must be finely pre-ground due to the crystal hardness. In order not to achieve too much of a cooling effect, the amount of dextrose is limited to less than 20%.

Fat-based pastes must be ground just like chocolate. The ingredients are blended – with the expectation of fat – in a mixer into a rollable dough. Subsequently they are rolled and lastly conched or mixed with the other fat.

The particle size must be as homogeneous as possible, whereby the maximum particle size may not exceed 35 µ. The smaller the particle size, the more stable the dispersion's behaviour. Interaction is created between the solid ingredients and the liquid oil as a result of which the oil settles on the surface of the solid ingredients. With a larger surface of solid ingredients, greater stabilising effect may be expected.

As already mentioned the crystallisation of fat in the paste is of the utmost importance, which implies that:
- we must quickly cool the paste thus creating small crystals; we prefer to use a blade heat exchanger;

NUT PASTES AND PRODUCTS

Praliné pastes

Although there is a clear difference between praliné and gianduja, both designations are often confused. Gianduja is a softly melting chocolate on the basis of almonds, hazelnuts or mixed nuts, which originally was an Italian speciality. Before we process gianduja, it must be melted and precrystallised. Gianduja is actually chocolate to which 20-25% nut puree has been added, whilst praliné is a soft, thick, liquid unctuous paste. In order to process praliné in pralines, cocoa butter or chocolate must be added to achieve consistency, without which the praliné will remain soft and difficult to process in bonbons.

The designation praliné is also fairly confusing since in some countries (such as Belgium, Germany and Switzerland) bonbons are typically referred to as pralines. In France, on the other hand, only bonbons in which praliné is processed, are referred to as pralines. It is therefore obvious to refer to praliné paste. In France it is called pâte pralinée. In Germany Nougatmasse, gianduja has a specific composition laid down in legislation.

Praliné pastes are used frequently since they are appreciated and provide numerous creative application options for the patisserie-chocolaterie industry. Praliné pralines also have a long shelf life. They could be used as fillings for moulded bonbons, for cutting bonbons or as flavouring for all manner of creams as well as ice cream. Praliné paste has quite a long shelf life and can be easily kept for 6 to 10 months. Over time, however, sediment settles resulting from the dry heavier particles slowly sinking to the bottom and sometimes leaving a dry hard crust on the bottom of the container.

The most popular praliné paste is made with hazelnuts, due to the low price of the nuts, their high fat content and their typical and powerful aroma. We are nonetheless able to create praliné pastes using all manner of nuts, or mixed nuts as long as they contain enough oil. In some pralinés (in which primarily other nuts are used), extra oil is added during production in order to achieve the correct unctuous paste as in hazelnut praliné.

Praliné created using Robot Coupe

TRUFFLES

Fast filling and sealing of truffle shells

Truffle shells are widely known and are available from several suppliers. They are designed to make life easier; even a layman is able to fill the hollow shells with cream, puree or ganache. Although these hollow shells are not cheap, they were actually especially developed to save time and hence also high labour costs, as a result of which, after working out the difference between the purchase price and the time saved by working more efficiently and faster, the scales should tip in favour of the professional. The company that years ago initially marketed these hollow shells, was so inventive that it also provided its customers with the opportunity to purchase two templates, resulting in the filling and sealing of the hollow shells taking place quickly and efficiently.

In the meantime many other producers of hollow shells have appeared on the market, selling the hollow shells but not the templates. As a result the filling of these moulds without the relevant templates does not save much time and the implementation of this originally fantastic concept proves to be fairly expensive. Unfortunately these templates are not very well-known and there is a certain risk involved in buying them from one manufacturer and using them on the hollow shells purchased from a competitor. The distance and the diameter of the holes differ from one manufacturer to the other. Under normal circumstances the supplier should provide two templates each with a different hole diameter.

The smallest holes are used to pipe the filling with a fast continuous motion into the shells. The template is subsequently scraped clean and carefully lifted and removed from the shell moulds. The filling's surface is then given a few hours' time to slightly crust.

Subsequently the second template with the slightly smaller holes is carefully placed on the surface of the (in the meantime slightly crusted) shell hole. It is now easy to seal all shells with chocolate. After crystallisation of the chocolate caps, all that is left to do is garnish the truffles creatively.

Strawberries-ginger truffles

Aw: 0.659

100 g cream	Blend all ingredients, except the chocolate.
200 g strawberry paste	
20 g ginger	Heat the mixture to 104°C.
80 g sorbitol	
20 g dextrose	Allow to fully cool before folding in the precrystallised chocolate.
50 g glucose	
20 g butter	Immediately pipe into hollow truffle shells.
570 g dark chocolate 36% CB	
	Allow to stiffen sufficiently before sealing the moulds.
	Garnish.

Banana
with Earl Grey truffles

Aw: 0.699

100 g water
10 g Earl Grey tea
250 g Boiron banana puree
150 g sucrose
60 g glucose
30 g glycerol
0.5 g Maldon salt
60 g milk chocolate

Bring the water to the boil. For strong tea, allow the tea to brew until the water has reached room temperature.

Strain the infusion and mix with puree, sucrose, glucose, glycerol and salt. Heat to 104°C.

Allow to fully cool before adding the precrystallised chocolate.

Immediately pipe into hollow chocolate truffle shells.

Seal the shells as soon as the filling has stiffened sufficiently.

Coat the shells with a thin layer of chocolate and garnish.

Cardamom-
olive oil-honey truffles

Aw: 0.455

100 g cream
100 g honey
50 g glucose
80 g maltodextrin
1 g Maldon salt
4 g ground cardamom
80 g glycerol
30 g olive oil
340 g milk chocolate

Blend all ingredients, except the olive oil and chocolate, and bring to the boil. If necessary, strain and allow to fully cool.

Mix the olive oil and the precrystallised chocolate and add to the mixture.

Immediately pipe into hollow shells.

Close the shells as soon as possible, coat with chocolate and garnish.

Rhubarb truffles

Aw: 0.695

---

250 g Boiron rhubarb puree
150 g sucrose
50 g glucose
chilli powder (alternative), as needed
40 g glycerol
60 g milk chocolate
dark chocolate
cacao powder

Heat the puree with the sucrose, glucose and chilli powder to 108°C.

Add the glycerol.

Fold the precrystallised chocolate into the cooled mixture.

Immediately pipe the filling in the shape of a ball using a smooth tip.

Close the shells and finish with a mixture of dark and white chocolate.

Lime-wasabi truffles

Aw: 0.520

100 g cream
80 g maltodextrin
20 g lime juice
wasabi powder, as needed
(depending on the quality
and strength of the wasabi)
100 g glycerol
50 g glucose
100 g invert sugar
1 g Maldon salt
340 g white chocolate
chocolate

Blend all ingredients, except the chocolate, and bring to the boil.

Allow to fully cool before folding in the precrystallised chocolate.

Immediately pipe into the truffle shells.

Close the shells as soon as possible, coat with chocolate and garnish.

Truffles
with raspberry puree

Aw: 0.676

----

500 g Boiron raspberry puree
100 g sucrose
50 g maltodextrin
70 g glucose
70 g sorbitol
0.6 g tabasco
0.5 g fleur de sel

Mix all ingredients and heat to 106°C.

Allow to fully cool.

Pipe into hollow shell moulds.

Seal the moulds after stiffening and garnish.

Coffee ganache

Aw: 0.678

300 g cream
20 g ground coffee
180 g glucose
100 g maltodextrin
50 g butter
80 g glycerol
2 g Maldon salt
700 g milk chocolate

Bring the cream, coffee, glucose, maltodextrin, butter, glycerol and salt to the boil.

Spread a thin film of chocolate on a rhodoid sheet and immediately place an 8 mm-10 mm frame in the chocolate while the latter is still liquid.

Allow to fully cool before pouring mixture into a prepared frame. Smooth out evenly.

Cut into the desired size and coat with milk chocolate.

Coffee gianduja

Aw: 0.555

80 g pure hazelnut puree
400 g milk chocolate
120 g hazelnut praline pasta
(see page 77)
120 g butter
15 g ground coffee

Combine the hazelnut puree and the precrystallised chocolate and add the praliné.

Lastly, fold in the butter and coffee.

Spread a thin film of chocolate on a rhodoid sheet and immediately place on an 8-mm frame in the milk chocolate while the latter is still liquid.

Pour the filling into the frame as soon as the chocolate has set.

Leave the filling to stiffen sufficiently before slicing it using a cutting guitar.

Coat with milk chocolate.

Garnish.

Nutty

Aw: 0.335

dark chocolate
500 g hazelnut praliné 50/50[7]
300 g milk chocolate
150 g bresilienne[8]

Spread a thin layer or dark chocolate on a rhodoid sheet.
Press an 8-mm frame into the chocolate while the latter is still liquid.

Blend the praliné with the milk chocolate and add the bresilienne.

Pour the mixture into the frame and smooth out evenly.
Allow to thoroughly crystallise.

Spread dark chocolate on the surface. Dab on the surface as soon
as the chocolate begins to thicken.

Leave to slightly crystallise before slicing using a cutting guitar.

Dip into dark chocolate to the rim.

7   Praliné: see Praliné pastes on page 77.

8   Bresilienne: see page 80.

Palet d'or
with long shelf life

Aw: 0.689

---

300 g cream
150 g glucose
100 g maltodextrin
50 g butter
40 g glycerol
80 g dextrose
20 g sorbitol
2 g Maldon salt
800 g dark chocolate 70%
Gold chips (PCB DC074)

Bring the cream, glucose, maltodextrin, butter, glycerol, dextrose, sorbitol and salt to the boil.

Allow to fully cool before folding in the precrystallised chocolate.

Various finishing options:

1) Using a rubber template (PCB Ref. PRO6A) stencil chocolate circles on which to pipe the ball-shaped fillings using a smooth tip measuring approximately 8 mm. Place a 1-cm bar on either side of the piped sheet. Cover the balls with a silicone sheet and a slab. Slightly press the slab against the levelling guides, to give all balls the same thickness. Remove the slab and allow the bonbons to thoroughly stiffen before removing the silicone.

2) Pour the filling into a frame and allow to stiffen thoroughly. Cut out circles using a round bonbon cutter. Provide them with a thin chocolate bottom (see *Fine Chocolates 2*, page 52).

3) Spread a thin layer of chocolate on a rhodoid sheet. Place a frame in the chocolate while the latter is still liquid. Pour the ganache into the frame after the chocolate has thoroughly stiffened. Leave to sufficiently harden before slicing in the desired size using a cutting guitar.

Allow the fillings to reach room temperature before covering them with dark chocolate.

With the help of a brush immediately sprinkle a few gold specks on the liquid chocolate and immediately cover with a rhodoid sheet.

Leave the rhodoid sheet on the crystallised chocolate as long as possible in order to maximise gloss (at least a half day).

Pistachio ganache

Aw: 0.654

320 g cream
50 g invert sugar
60 g glycerol
60 g dextrose
130 g butter
150 g pistachio puree (Pregel)
820 g white chocolate
dark chocolate

Bring the cream, invert sugar, glycerol, dextrose, butter and pistachio puree to the boil.

Allow to fully cool before pouring onto the precrystallised chocolate.

Spread the mixture in a prepared frame.

Cut in the desired size and cover with dark chocolate.

Decoration: use the flexible section of drinking straws.
Press into the chocolate, while the latter is still liquid.
Remove only after the chocolate has crystallised sufficiently.

Pistachio cubes

Aw: 0.697

128

100 g butter
460 g marzipan 50/50
90 g pistachio puree (Pregel)
70 g coarsely chopped pistachio nuts
100 g milk chocolate
100 g dark chocolate 36% CB

Combine the butter and the marzipan.

Add the puree and the chopped pistachios.

Lastly, fold in both precrystallised chocolates.

Warning! Ensure that the marzipan, butter and puree are whipped into a creamy mixture before adding the chocolates. Do not blend longer than necessary.

Spread a thin film of chocolate on a rhodoid sheet and immediately place a 6-mm frame on the chocolate while the latter is still liquid.

After the chocolate has stiffened, smooth out the filling evenly in the frame and put in the cooler.

Slice the cold slab using a cutting guitar.

Allow to reach room temperature before coating the cubes with chocolate.

Sunny

Recipe 1   *Aw: 0.666*

100 g cream	Blend all ingredients, except the chocolate, and bring to the boil.
4 g dried lavender	
80 g glucose	Leave to fully cool.
60 g sorbitol	
60 g dextrose	Strain the cream onto the precrystallised chocolate.
80 g butter	
520 g chocolate 36% CB	

Alternative: Recipe 2: with anise liqueur   *Aw: 0.752*

100 g cream	Proceed as in recipe 1 and add the liqueur after the chocolate is blended.
3 g dried lavender	
80 g glucose	Spread a thin film of chocolate on a rhodoid sheet and place a 6-mm frame
50 g sorbitol	on the chocolate while the latter is still liquid.
50 g dextrose	
120 g butter	Pour the ganache into the frame as soon as the chocolate has stiffened.
520 g chocolate 36% CB	
50 g anise liqueur	Leave to set sufficiently before slicing using a cutting guitar.
	Dip into dark chocolate and garnish.

Amandine

500 g praliné paste 50/50
250 g dark chocolate 36% CB[9]

[Or, if a slightly less sweet recipe
is desired:
500 g pure hazelnut puree[10]
550 g dark chocolate 36% CB
(or 600 g milk chocolate
or 650 g white chocolate)

marzipan

Blend the praliné paste (or hazelnut puree) with the precrystallised chocolate.

Pour into a 3-mm frame and smooth out evenly. Allow to stiffen.
In the meantime roll a slice of plain or coloured marzipan into a 4-mm slab.

With the help of a little liqueur or thin sugar syrup adhere the marzipan
to the unmoulded praliné. Turn over.

Roll out a second slice of marzipan into a 3-mm slab and place on praliné.

Garnish with decorative piping.

Spread a thin layer of cocoa butter on the surface in order to prevent
the marzipan from drying too quickly.

Allow to rest for at least one hour before slicing the slab using a cutting guitar,
since the moisture used to apply the marzipan, must be given the opportunity
to penetrate into the marzipan. Otherwise the marzipan will separate from
the praliné.

---

9   The amount of chocolate to be added depends on the following factors:
   - The percentage of cocoa butter in the chocolate.
   - If milk or white chocolate is used, account must be taken of the percentage of milk fat in the chocolate.
   - The free fat content in the praliné.
   - The size of the nut particles (grain size). Example: an industrially produced praliné has, due to its machine grinding, a finer grain size than a home-made praliné. The larger the nut particle, the less nut surface, and the less free oil. In this case less chocolate must be added to the recipe, otherwise the mixture becomes too hard and uncuttable.

   In a finely grained praliné (below 30 μ) the addition of 50% dark chocolate (with 36% cocoa butter content) will yield a softly melting and easily sliceable result. When using milk chocolate 60% must be added in order to achieve the same pleasant softly melting and easily sliceable praliné. And when using white chocolate 70% must be added. The option exists to use only cocoa butter instead of chocolate, in order to decrease sweetness. In this case approximately 20% is sufficient.

10   Pure hazelnut puree is made of (dark) roasted hazelnuts, ground into a liquid pulp. The same comments apply here as in the previous footnote.

Coconut

Aw: 0.646

100 g coconut milk
50 g invert sugar
50 g glycerol
50 g dextrose
1 g Maldon salt
50 g butter
50 g grated coconut
550 g milk chocolate
25 g rum 54%
dark chocolate

Blend all ingredients (except the chocolate and liqueur) and bring to the boil.

Allow the cream to fully cool before folding it into the precrystallised chocolate.

Add the liqueur.

Pour into a 5-mm frame and leave to fully crystallise before slicing using a cutting guitar.

Coat with dark chocolate.

Vanilla and raspberries

First layer   *Aw: 0.690*

12 g pectin
500 g sucrose
500 g raspberry puree (Bourbon)
110 g glucose
6 g tartaric acid
10 g water (maximum)

Combine the pectin and sucrose.

Blend the puree with the pectin-sucrose mixture and the glucose and heat to 107 °C.

Dissolve the tartaric acid in the water and add to the mixture at the end of the cooking process.

Immediately pour into a 4-mm frame on a Silpat mat.

Second layer   *Aw: 0.672*

100 g sucrose
60 g cream
50 g sweetened condensed milk
190 g glucose
25 g invert sugar
25 g inulin
25 g glycerol
375 g butter
550 g white chocolate
1 g vanilla flavouring
dark chocolate

Bring the sucrose, cream, sweetened condensed milk, glucose, invert sugar, inulin, glycerol and butter to the boil.

Allow to fully cool before folding in the precrystallised chocolate.

Add the flavouring.

Place a 4-mm frame on the first layer and immediately pour the ganache on the fruit dough.

Leave to stiffen sufficiently before covering with a thin layer of chocolate.

Turn upside down and cut using a cutting guitar.

Coat with dark chocolate and garnish.

Limon ganache
with orange blossom
marzipan

First layer   *Aw: depends on marzipan*

marzipan
orange blossom flavouring

Flavour the marzipan with the orange blossom flavouring

Roll out the marzipan into a 3-mm slab.

Place the marzipan in an 8-mm frame.

Second layer   *Aw: 0.664*

250 g cream
40 g glucose
20 g glycerol
50 g invert sugar
25 g maltodextrin
50 g Boiron lemon purée
1 g Maldon salt
250 g melt chocolate
dark chocolate

Heat the cream, glucose, glycerol, invert sugar, maltodextrin, lemon puree
and salt to 107°C.

Allow to fully cool before pouring onto the precrystallised chocolate.

Fill the frame and carefully smooth out the surface.

Leave to stiffen sufficiently before creating a thin bottom with the chocolate.

Cut in the desired size.

Coat with dark chocolate.

Bilberry duo

First layer *Aw: 0.643*

---

9 g pectin (yellow)
375 g sucrose
375 g bilberry puree (Bourbon)
120 g glucose
20 g lemon juice

Blend the pectin with the sucrose and subsequently add the puree and glucose.

Heat to 104°C. Add the lemon juice.

Mix thoroughly and immediately pour the mixture into a 4-mm frame on a Silpat mat.

Second layer *Aw: 0.656*

---

75 g sweetened condensed milk
18 g maltodextrin
25 g glycerol
75 g glucose
20 g invert sugar
150 g butter
300 g dark chocolate

Bring the sweetened condensed milk, maltodextrin, glycerol, glucose and invert sugar to the boil. Allow to fully cool.

In the meantime soften the butter and beat in the food processor.

Trickle the syrup onto the butter in the slowly rotating processor.

Stir in the precrystallised chocolate.

Place a 4-mm frame on the first layer and fill with ganache.

Spread a thin layer of chocolate on the surface as soon as the ganache has stiffened sufficiently. Allow to stiffen again and turn upside down.

Spread an even layer of dark chocolate on the surface and immediately sprinkle 'Paillettes Croustillantes Dorées' from PCB[11] on the chocolate while the latter is still liquid.

When ready slice using a cutting guitar.

---

11 Decoration alternatives:
- Mix coarse granulated sugar with red-coloured cocoa butter. Add a few gold sequins (PCB ref. DC074) and knead thoroughly using both hands until the sugar is evenly coloured.
- Flavoured sugar: In the food processor grind coarse granulated sugar with lemon and/or orange peels into small evenly distributed particles. Sieve if necessary and subsequently store in sealed jars.

Cassis

First layer   *Aw: 0.643*

6 g pectin (yellow) 250 g sucrose 250 g cassis puree (Boiron) 80 g glucose	Combine the pectin and the sucrose and add the puree and glucose. Heat to 103°C. Immediately pour the mixture into a 4-mm frame on a Silpat mat.

Second layer   *Aw: 0.478*

50 g cream 50 g glycerol 50 g dextrose 1 g Maldon salt 50 g honey 50 g butter 340 g milk chocolate or 340 g dark chocolate	Blend all ingredients (except the chocolate) and bring to the boil. Allow to fully cool before folding in the precrystallised chocolate. Place a 4-mm frame on the first layer in which to spread the ganache. Allow to crystallise before slicing the slab using a cutting guitar. Coat with dark chocolate.

Cardamom

First layer   *Aw: 0.662*

_____

175 g butter	Stir the butter until smooth. Add the precrystallised chocolate and the oil.
450 g dark chocolate 30%	
50 g olive oil	Spread a very thin layer of chocolate on a rhodoid sheet.

Immediately place a 4-mm frame in the chocolate while the latter is still liquid.

Leave the chocolate to crystallise before pouring the ganache on it.

Smooth out evenly and allow to set.

Second layer   *Aw: 0.695*

_____

150 g cream
4 g cardamom powder
0.5 g Maldon salt
30 g glycerol
25 g dextrose
410 g white chocolate

Blend all ingredients, except the chocolate and bring this mixture to the boil.

Leave to fully cool before folding in the precrystallised chocolate.

Place a 4 mm-frame on the first layer in which to immediately spread the ganache.

Leave to sufficiently crystallise before unmoulding.

Slice in the desired size using a cutting guitar.

Lime

First layer   *Aw: 0.647*

150 g raisins
50 g rum 54°
1 g allspice
40 g dextrose
200 g butter
620 g milk chocolate
40 g glycerol

Blend the raisins, liqueur, spices and dextrose into a paste in a food processor.

Soften the butter and mix with the precrystallised chocolate; add the glycerol.

Spread a thin layer of precrystallised chocolate on a rhodoid sheet
and immediately cover with a 4-mm frame.

Spread the filling in the frame and leave to crystallise before topping
with a second 4-mm frame in which the second layer is to be spread.

Second layer   *Aw: 0.763*

400 g cream
lime zest
20 g lime juice
1 laurel leaf
1 g dried juniper berries
40 g glycerol
50 g dextrose
50 g invert sugar
80 g butter
640 g milk chocolate
dark chocolate

Blend all ingredients (without the chocolate) and bring to the boil.

Allow the mixture to fully cool before straining it onto
the precrystallised chocolate.

Fold into the homogeneous ganache and pour into a frame over the first layer.

Allow to crystallise sufficiently before slicing using a cutting guitar.

Coat with dark chocolate.

MOULDED PRALINES

Blueberry

Aw: 0.676

100 g cream
100 g sucrose
80 g glucose
120 g blueberry puree
50 g sorbitol
0.2 g citric acid or 4.5 g lemon juice
100 g white chocolate

Bring the cream, sucrose, glucose, blueberry puree and sorbitol to the boil. Add the citric acid or lemon juice and continue to heat to 108°C.

Allow to fully cool before folding in the chocolate.

Pipe into chocolate moulds.

Green tea

Aw: 0.689

300 g cream
160 g glucose
2 g Maldon salt
14 g green tea powder
100 g maltodextrin
30 g butter
70 g glycerol
400 g milk chocolate

Bring cream, glucose, salt, tea powder, maltodextrin, butter and glycerol to the boil.

Allow to fully cool before folding in the precrystallised chocolate.

Immediately pour into chocolate moulds.

Seal the moulds as soon as the filling has stiffened sufficiently.

Cocktail with coconut

Aw: 0.473

80 g sucrose
75 g glucose
80 g coconut puree
80 g puree of cranberries
and cherries (Boiron)
40 g butter
25 g dextrose
40 g glycerol
1 g Maldon salt
30 g grated coconut flakes
40 g white chocolate

Heat the sucrose, glucose, both purees, butter, dextrose, glycerol and salt to 107°C.

Fold the coconut flakes into the syrup.

Allow to fully cool before stirring in the chocolate. Use a whisk instead of a spatula.

Immediately pipe into the moulds.

Strawberry
and cinnamon duo

Aw: 0.530

Strawberry sauce
100 g cream
1.5 g cinnamon
100 g glycerol
100 g dextrose
2 g Maldon salt
90 g invert sugar
100 g butter
330 g milk chocolate
240 g dark chocolate

Pipe one third of the strawberry sauce into the moulds.

Bring the cream, cinnamon, glycerol, dextrose, salt, invert sugar and butter to the boil. Leave to fully cool before folding in the precrystallised chocolate.

Pipe the ganache onto the strawberry sauce and allow to slightly crystallise before closing the moulds.

Strawberry sauce   *Aw: 0.676*

500 g strawberry puree (Boiron)
100 g sucrose
50 g inulin
50 g dextrose
50 g maltodextrin
60 g sorbitol
0.6 g Tabasco

Blend all ingredients and heat to 104°C.

Caramel and banana duo

Balsamic caramel   *Aw: 0.599*

---

200 g sucrose
85 g balsamico
80 g butter
1 g Maldon salt

Caramelise the sucrose to a medium brown colour.

Carefully quench with the balsamico and immediately add the butter and salt.

Leave to fully cool.

Pipe the caramel into chocolate shells to one third the height.

Banana ganache   *Aw: 0.698*

---

480 g banana puree (Boiron)
200 g sucrose
80 g dextrose
100 g honey
90 g glycerol
500 g milk chocolate

Bring the puree and the sucrose, dextrose, honey and glycerol to the boil.

Leave to fully cool before folding into the precrystallised chocolate.

Immediately pipe the ganache on the caramel.

Allow to stiffen sufficiently before sealing the moulds.

Raspberry ganache

Aw: 0.694

250 g Boiron raspberry puree
150 g sucrose
50 g glucose
15 g lime juice
35 g glycerol
200 g dark chocolate

Heat the raspberry puree, sucrose, glucose, lime juice and glycerol to 107°C.

Allow to cool to room temperature before folding in the precrystallised chocolate.

Immediately pipe into the chocolate moulds.

Leave to stiffen sufficiently before sealing the moulds.

Guava Rosa

Aw: 0.528

100 g cream
50 g 'Guava Rosa' (Pregel)
100 g glycerol
100 g dextrose
2 g Maldon salt
80 g invert sugar
100 g butter
400 g dark chocolate
coloured cocoa butter

Blend all ingredients except the chocolate and bring to the boil.

Allow to fully cool before folding in the precrystallised chocolate.

Place the unmoulded pralines in the freezer for approximately 5 minutes.

Subsequently spray a light mist of coloured cocoa butter over the pralines.

Coconut with bilberries

First layer   *Aw: 0.694*

500 g bilberry puree (Boiron)	Heat the puree, sucrose, glucose and lemon juice to 105°C.
300 g sucrose	
100 g glucose	Add the sorbitol and allow to cool to room temperature.
20 g lemon juice	
50 g sorbitol	Fold in the precrystallised chocolate.
300 g milk chocolate	
	Immediately pipe into the chocolate shells to mid-height.

Second layer   *Aw: 0.591*

100 g cream	Blend all ingredients except the chocolate and bring to the boil.
90 g coconut paste (Pregel)	
100 g glycerol	Leave the mixture to fully cool before folding in the precrystallised chocolate.
120 g glucose	
3 g Maldon salt	Immediately pipe onto the first layer.
80 g butter	
280 g white chocolate	Close the moulds after the filling has slightly crystallised.

Matcha

Aw: 0.482

———

100 g cream
12 g matcha green tea powder
100 g glycerol
100 g dextrose
3 g Maldon salt
100 g invert sugar
80 g butter
200 g milk chocolate
200 g white chocolate

Blend all ingredients except the chocolates.

Bring the mixture to the boil.

Allow to fully cool before folding in the precrystallised chocolates.

Immediately pipe into chocolate shells.

Seal the moulds as soon as the ganache has stiffened sufficiently.

Sesame praline

Aw: 0.400

100 g sucrose
30 g roasted sesame seeds
100 g almonds or
200 g almond praliné 50/50
1 g Maldon salt
50 g milk chocolate

Caramelise the sucrose and pour the caramel onto a Silpat mat.

Roast the sesame seeds.

Break the caramel into chunks as soon as it is cooled.

Grind the caramel and the almonds into a fine, smooth liquid paste.

Fold the sesame seeds into the praliné.

Immediately pipe into chocolate moulds.

Allow to stiffen sufficiently before sealing the moulds with chocolate.

Tonka beans

Aw: 0.699

—————

50 g sucrose
30 g condensed milk
10 g maltodextrose
10 g glycerol
85 g glucose
10 g invert sugar
150 g butter
260 g dark chocolate
tonka flavouring[13], as needed

Bring the sucrose, condensed milk, maltodextrose, glycerol, glucose and invert sugar to the boil.

Allow the syrup to fully cool.

In the meantime soften the butter.

In the food processor slowly add the cooled syrup to the butter at low speed.

Fold the precrystallised chocolate and flavouring into the ganache.

Pour a double quantity of shallow chocolate moulds.

Unmould half the moulds after hardening.

Pipe the ganache into balls in the chocolate shells. Immediately seal with the chocolate shells.

Allow to stiffen sufficiently before unmoulding.

—————————————————————

13 The use of tonka beans is banned in most countries due to the high coumarin content.
The Belgian Food and Drugs Act, however, allows for the infusion of tonka beans,
but the bean's dry matter may not be processed.
Coumarin is an anticoagulant, which may be lethal in large doses. Coumarin not only appears
to be toxic, but it is also said to be a carcinogen. The tonka bean contains 10% coumarin,
which is just a 'copy' of the tonka aroma, without any of its ingredients.

Seashells

Aw: 0.688

125 g cream
100 g sweetened condensed milk
200 g sucrose
375 g glucose
50 g invert sugar
50 g inulin
50 g glycerol
750 g butter
1200 g dark chocolate
4 g Butterscotch flavouring

Bring cream, sweetened condensed milk, sucrose, glucose, invert sugar, inulin, glycerol and butter to the boil.

Allow to fully cool before folding in the precrystallised chocolate.

Add flavouring as needed.

Pour double the number of chocolate shells. Unmould half of the shells.

Pipe the ganache in the shape of a ball into the remaining chocolate shells.
Place the unmoulded shells on them in the shape of a fan. Allow to cool sufficiently before unmoulding.

Liquorice

Aw: 0.615

———

300 g cream	Bring the cream, liquorice, glucose and sucrose, salt, butter
Liquorice, as needed	and glycerol to the boil.
200 g glucose	
120 sucrose	Leave to fully cool.
2 g Maldon salt	
50 g butter	Strain onto the precrystallised chocolate.
90 g glycerol	
720 g milk chocolate	Immediately pipe into the moulds.

Allow to stiffen sufficiently before sealing the moulds with chocolate.

Jasmine

Aw: 0.700

300 g cream
150 g glucose
1 g Maldon salt
10 g jasmine tea[14]
110 g maltodextrin
40 g butter
70 g glycerol
470 g milk chocolate

Bring the cream, glucose, salt, jasmine tea, maltodextrin, butter and glycerol to the boil.

Allow to fully cool before straining the infusion onto the precrystallised chocolate. Mix and pipe into the chocolate moulds.

Seal the moulds as soon as the filling has stiffened sufficiently.

---

14   Dried jasmine flowers are fairly expensive, which is why dried jasmine is frequently combined with Chinese tea, which results in a totally different flavour profile.
Pure jasmine flowers look like small dried balls, which open in hot water, whereby the long flower petals unroll.

Coconut

Aw: 0.572

Base

80 g roasted sesame seeds 200 g milk chocolate 40 g pure hazelnut puree	Combine the sesame seeds. Combine the pure hazelnut puree and the precrystallised chocolate and fold in the cooled sesame seeds. Spread a 4-mm layer on a rhodoid sheet and allow to set. Cut out circles with a diameter of approximately 20 mm. arrange half the circles on a sheet of greaseproof paper (see *Fine Chocolates 2*, page 53). The other half will be used as the top of the bonbons.

Filling

250 g butter 1000 g milk chocolate 100 g glycerol 4 g coconut flavouring 50 g grated coconut milk chocolate	Soften the butter. Fold in the precrystallised chocolate. Lastly add the glycerol, flavouring and coconut. Pipe this mixture in ball shapes onto the bases and paste the leftover circles diagonally on the ganache. Allow to stiffen sufficiently before coating with liquid milk chocolate.

Violette

Aw: 0.570

Bottom

---

80 g roasted sesame seeds
200 g milk chocolate
40 g pure hazelnut puree

Roast the sesame seeds.

Blend the precrystallised chocolate and the pure hazelnut puree
and fold in the cooled sesame seeds.

Spread a 4-mm thick layer on a rhodoid sheet and allow to set.

Cut circles with a diameter of approximately 20 mm and as many
with a diameter of 10 mm. Arrange and secure (see *Fine Chocolates 2*, page 53).

---

250 g butter
750 g milk chocolate
50 g glycerol
2 g violette flavouring

Soften the butter and fold in the precrystallised chocolate.

Add the glycerol and flavouring.

Pipe in the shape of a ball on the bases and place a small circle atop.

Allow to stiffen sufficiently before coating with liquid dark chocolate.

Lavender

Aw: 0.417

0.5 g powdered lavender
200 g milk chocolate
40 g pure hazelnut puree
10 g butter
0.5 g lavender flavouring

Grind the dried lavender into powder. Strain the powder and use only the finest residue.

Blend the chocolate and the hazelnut puree, add the butter, powder and flavouring.

With the help of a round or oval rubber template (PCB ref. round: PRO 6A, oval: P002A) spread chocolate on a transfer sheet.

Repeat on a rhodoid sheet or on greaseproof paper.

Using a star tip, pipe rosettes on the chocolate slices.

Turn over the transfer sheet with the chocolate slices and press them onto the rosettes while the latter are still soft.

Baked marzipan

Aw: 0.380

Roll out marzipan between two 12-mm rods.

Use a Köningsberger marzipan cutter[16] to cut out the shapes.

Arrange on baking tray. Slightly colour the top on a gas burner or briefly bake in 220°C oven.

Fill the holes with raspberry jam.

Raspberry jam   *Aw: 0.752* [17]

250 g Boiron raspberry jam puree
150 g sucrose
50 g glucose
10 g lime juice
25 g glycerol

Blend all ingredients and heat to 107°C.

16 The Köningsberger marzipan cutter is a special tool that cuts the marzipan as well as the hole in the middle. To be purchased from Dedy Gmbh. See http://www.Dedy.de
17 The raspberry jam releases moisture to the marzipan during storage, providing a moisture balance between both for excellent storage. If the marzipan is baked, the Aw drops dramatically.

IV

Appendices

Why does chocolate turn darker when you pour water on it?

The reason is twofold:
* Chocolate is a suspension of solid particles in a fat phase. Its microstructure changes when a liquid is added and it turns into an emulsion (water in fat), thus altering the light reflex and colour.
* The dry fat-free cocoa absorbs water and hence its light reflection changes (decreases) and becomes darker.

Why does chocolate thicken when moisture is added?

Because you create an emulsion from water in fat. The drops of aqueous liquid increase viscosity.

Why doesn't chocolate melt or melt with great difficulty when exposed too long to light?

Moisture absorption results in the polymerisation of the proteins, which form a skeleton on the surface, as it were. Especially chocolate shavings have a large surface area and are rapidly prone to external factors (moisture, light, air and odours). That is why shavings must be thoroughly packaged immediately after use. Hollow figures and other chocolate items with a large surface area must be exposed as little as possible to the afore-mentioned factors.

How does a refractometer work?

A refractometer is an instrument to measure substances dissolved in water.

The refractometer uses the principle of light reflection by liquids. Since light travelling from the air through a liquid, is slowed down, this phenomenon produces a 'break' in the water, which is partially saturated. In a nutshell, the more dissolved substances, the more breaks and the higher the refraction index.

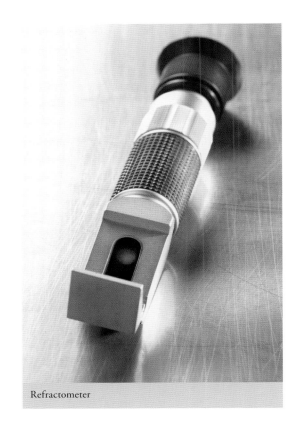

Refractometer

What is curdling?

This is the separation of an emulsion of two liquids that do not mix. The most typical example is an emulsion of oil and water (e.g., mayonnaise). Reasons:
- Incorrect proportion of ingredients
- Incorrect mixing temperatures

Remedies (depending on the recipe):
- Homogenise using a handheld mixer or blender
- Add an emulsifier (in some cases a little lecithin helps)
- Add a thickener
- Allow to slightly solidify, then stir thoroughly (in processor where needed)

Why do milk products curdle when they come in contact with acids?

Milk is an emulsion of fat in water, stabilised by milk proteins. At a pH of 4.75 or lower the protein settles and loses its emulsifying properties resulting in curdling in a ganache, for example.

The pH can potentially be adjusted by using a buffer or a little sodium bicarbonate.

Is the use of colouring agents such as silver and gold innocuous?

Silver as a food additive (E174) is 99.5 % pure silver, which is used to colour some chocolate products and liqueurs. For chocolate products it is only to be used for external decoration. The quantities to be used are always minimal. Powdered silver in particular easily turns dull when in contact with air.

Gold as a food additive (E175) consists of 99.99% gold, where it is authorised to add up to 7% silver and 4% copper. These additions are intended to make the gold softer in order to allow it to be flattened into gold leaf. Gold mixed with copper, provides an orange hue, and when adding silver, a greenish hue. Gold leaf is only to be used for external decoration on chocolate products and in some liqueurs.

Watt is the difference between vanilla and vanillin?

Vanilla is the fruit of an orchid variety and originates in Mexico. The plant is currently also grown in Madagascar, Indonesia, Tahiti, Java, Mauritius, Sri Lanka, the Seychelles and Reunion. Bourbon vanilla comes from the island of Reunion (formerly Bourbon) near the east coast of Africa. Vanilla from Tahiti has a typical odour due to the presence of piperonal.

Vanilla is sold in various qualities and the decisive factors for the quality are moisture content, flavour, odour, appearance and oil content.

Vanillin is the best known and typical odour and flavouring in vanilla; the content is 2-5%, and the substance can be isolated by extraction. Currently vanillin is primarily produced synthetically. Ethylvanillin is approximately four times as strong as natural vanillin.

Vanillin is volatile and must be stored in sealed packaging. It is significantly cheaper than vanilla.

Antioxidants

Antioxidants protect products against chemical spoilage by oxygen. They protect fats against rancidity and prevent the discoloration of fruit, thus extending shelf life. By inhibiting oxidation, the creation of unpleasant odours and flavour degradation is also prevented.

Aromas

Aromas are odour and flavour enhancers added to give a product a specific flavour or odour or improve the natural flavour and odour. Since flavour and odour is seldom only made up of a single substance, mixtures of substances are often required.

Atom

This is the smallest particle of an element (e.g., He, O or C), which still has its specific properties. It consists of a nucleus surrounded by an electron cloud. Electrons are minute particles, which revolve in a course around the nucleus. The atom's nucleus has a positive load, and the electrons are negatively charged. The size of an atom is determined by the electron cloud.

Azo colouring agents

The name 'azo' comes from an atom group (azo group) with two nitrogen atoms bonded by a double bond. Azo colouring agents are synthetic dyes in which an azo group appears. They are the most frequently used colouring agents. Approximately 60-70% of all colouring agents in foodstuffs are azo dyes. Theoretically every colour can be made using azo dyes, but most applications are situated in the yellow/red and brown/blue area. Azo dyes are much more stable than most natural dyes. Azo dyes are stable at all pH values occurring in foodstuffs, are heat-stable and are fairly insensitive to air or oxygen, which allow azo dyes to be used in nearly all foodstuffs. The only disadvantage is that they are nearly insoluble in fat or oil. When these dyes settle on a carrier, e.g., silicic acid or aluminium oxide, it is the result of a very fine powder suspended in oil or fat. The acute toxicity of azo dyes is very low, in accordance with criteria laid down by the EU. Since the dyes are so strong, the required concentrations are also low. In order to ingest a lethal dose, one would have to eat more than 100 kilos of food coloured with azo dyes in one day.

Azo compounds used in foodstuffs are listed below. The E numbers refer to the authorised additives in the European Union.
- Amaranth (E123)
- Allura Red AC (E129)
- Azorubine (E122)
- Brown FK (E154) – mixture of 6 azo dyes
- Brown HT (E155)
- Brilliant black BN (E151)
- Cochineal red A (E124 - synthetic variant of the actual cochineal).
- Yellow 2G (E107).
- Sunset yellow FCF (E110).
- Lithol Rubine BK (E180).
- Red 2G (E128).
- Tartrazine (E102).
- Quinoline yellow (E104).

Base

Bases are substances with a pH value (degree of acidity) greater than 7 (not acid). See also below under 'Degree of acidity'.

Bloom

Unit of measure that determines the strength of gels measured using a Bloom gelometer.

Buffers

Buffers monitor the degree of acidity, emulsifiers stabilise emulsions, stabilisers take care of the rest. They are all substances that have all manner of stabilising effects, which span from the preservation of viscosity to maintaining the colour or aroma.

Caramelisation

Thermal polymerisation and degradation in alkaline environment, creating brown-coloured products and a typical aroma (see also 'Maillard reaction').

Carbohydrates

Carbohydrates occur in three groupings: monosaccharides, disaccharides and polysaccharides. All carbohydrates are made up of sugar. Monosaccharides of one sugar, disaccharides of two sugars and polysaccharides of an entire chain of sugars. All carbohydrates provide the same amount of energy: 4 kcal per gram. Fibres are also carbohydrates (see below under 'Dietary fibres).

CBE (Cocoa Butter Equivalent)

This is a fat with a structure that is very similar to that of cocoa butter.

Citric acids

Citric acids occur naturally in foodstuffs and the body, and have a multifaceted effect. They increase a product's acidity, enhance the effect of antioxidants and a number of preservatives and may have a colour-preserving effect.

Colloids

These are particles measuring between a few nanometres and a few micrometres. They are small enough to remain in suspension in a liquid without sinking to the bottom (see also 'Colloids' on page 41).

Colouring agents (E100-E180)

Colouring agents are used to colour a product or enhance, embellish or maintain the existing colour. Whilst the correct use of some additives such as preservatives is warranted in terms of food safety, the usefulness of colouring agents and flavour enhancers is up for discussion since in theory they are not necessary products with high-quality raw materials. Those who use these substances are often blamed for making products look better than they are in reality. There are three types of colouring agents: natural colouring agents (harvested from plants), nature-identical colouring agents (chemically synthesised substances, identical to those in nature) and synthetic colouring agents (chemically synthesised substances that do not occur in nature).

Creamy

This implies soft in the mouth, well bonded, fatty with a pleasant mouthfeel.

DE (Dextrose Equivalent)

This is the measure for the degree of hydrolysis (breakdown) of starch or the total number of reducing sugars (reducing capacity). The higher the DE value, the more starch is converted.

Dietary fibre

This is a collective noun for vegetable substances that are not digested or absorbed in the small intestine of the body, resulting in full or partial fermentation in the large intestine. Dietary fibre has a positive impact on the body, since it lowers cholesterol, promotes regularity and lowers the blood sugar level. Fibres are subdivided in two categories: soluble or fermentable fibres and insoluble or non-fermentable fibres.

Dispersion

Dispersion is a mixture of thickener with a solid or liquid substance or gas in a liquid. The liquid is most often water, whilst the dispersed substance is distributed in minute bubbles, but is not dissolved. A few examples:

Margarine is an emulsion of water droplets (dispersed) in fat (continuous)

Whipped cream is a foam of air bubbles (dispersed) in heavy cream (continuous). When beating the cream the air bubbles are whisked into the cream (dispersed), producing whipped cream.

in such a way that microorganisms are unable to or barely able to grow or survive in food, or be specifically lethal to microorganisms. Obviously the preservative should not be harmful to humans. The authorised substances in foodstuffs have, for the most part, an E number in the series 200 to 299. In addition, some substances have a preservative effect, but are not only used as preservatives. Examples include sugars in jams, salts for pickling and alcohol in drinks.

Probiotic

Food supplement with specific live, health-promoting microorganisms, namely (lactic acid) bacteria, with a potential positive impact on health in general and the digestive process in particular. A few of these influences are scientifically proven and accepted (inhibiting diarrhoea, remedying/decreasing lactose intolerance, improving transit), whilst other positive effects are not considered to be proven.

Proteins

Proteins or egg whites consist of long chains of various (some 500 on average) amino acids bonded to each other. Amino acids are therefore essential to our body's proper functioning. Proteins are used in the body to build muscles. Enzymes are also proteins. In general proteins may have a limited emulsifying effect. Amino acids not converted into enzymes, are converted into energy.

Relative humidity

Relative humidity is defined as the ratio indicating how much water vapour is contained in the air at a prescribed temperature compared to the maximum quantity contained in a specific air quantity (at that temperature). A value of 100% shows a maximum quantity of water vapour: the air is saturated. For a relative humidity of 50% the air contains half of the maximum possible quantity of water vapour at the prevailing temperature. At 100% condensation and drop formation is initiated.

RDI

Stands for **R**ecommended **D**aily **I**ntake, which is the daily amount of a specific substance to be ingested by an average adult (e.g., vitamin C) in order for the body to function normally. This indication is therefore not the same for everyone and is only an indication for a person's RDI. Physical activity, age and other factors affect the RDI.

Stabilisers

These are substances that slow down or inhibit chemical reactions. They are often added to slightly binding substance to extend their shelf life or make them easier to transport. Stabilisers ensure that the blend of two non-miscible substances is maintained and can, for example, be applied to products that are difficult to mix and that still require a few steps in the production process.

Stabilisers are related to buffing agents and emulsifiers. They also ensure that the status of the foodstuffs to which they are added changes as little as possible.

Starch

Starch is a polysaccharide primarily occurring in potatoes, wheat and maize. It is also found in legumes, tuberous vegetables and a number of other plants. It represents an energy reserve for those plants. After opening the plant cells the starch is released, which after a few washings settles as a white powder. This substance consists of a long dextrose chain. Before the energy can be garnered from the starch, the starch must be broken down into sugar, which requires the necessary time. Starch is an example of a 'slow sugar' and will only deliver energy to the body after a few hours. Starch stiffens at high temperatures.

Starch gelatinisation

The starch molecules lose their molecular order in the presence of water and at high temperatures. They leave the starch grain, forming a gel, which is called starch gelatinisation.

Sterilised milk

Sterilisation also kills all microorganisms and takes place by heating the milk for a few seconds with steam to 130°C and subsequently heating it for 10-20 minutes to 110-120°C. This milk can be kept at room temperature for a few months.

Sucrose

Sucrose is regular sugar. It is a disaccharide, consisting of a glucose unit and a fructose unit.

Surface tension (interface tension)

This is the repelling force to another phase and the attraction to its own phase.

Taste and flavour paring

The science that deals with the examination of similarities between two substances. For example, studies have shown that if two substances have several equal flavour components (molecules), they will harmonise well with each other. The more matching flavour properties they display, the better they can be combined with each other.

Thickeners

Also referred to as gelling agent. Thickeners are a group of substances, nearly always carbohydrates, which are able to bind water and hence thicken a product.

Transfats

Transfats are produced by the hardening of edible oil in order to improve preservation and processing properties. Transfats can practically not be broken down by the human body. This consumed fat settles in the body, primarily in the stomach area. Other designations for transfats are: partially hardened fat or hydrogenated fat. These fats are found in biscuits, deep-fried products and some crisps.

UHT

This acronym stands for **U**ltra-**H**igh **T**emperature and refers to the way in which milk is sterilised. UHT milk is heated for 2 to 5 seconds to 135-150°C in order to kill all microorganisms. This milk can be kept unopened at room temperature for three months.

Water activity

Indicates the amount of free water available (to microorganisms). The 'free' water is expressed in the Aw value. Molecules and ions in food bind with water, which makes it unavailable to other reactions. Free water is not bound and is therefore available.

Due to a availability of free water, microbial growth or chemical breakdown reaction may occur. Microorganisms prefer the concentration of dissolved substances in their cell not to differ too much from the concentration outside their cell. With differences that are too great the cell wall breaks down and the cell snaps. This is due to the fact that the water always travels to the location with the highest concentration of substances. If a cell is placed in a concentrated solution, it will just be drained since it receives no water, even if it finds itself in the middle of it. It is also unable to grow, since even if there is water, it is not available (active). This availability can even be reduced if substances are in the vicinity that bind with water, such as proteins, sugars, salts, fibres and binding agents. Free water and bound water together represent the total water content.

Whey proteins

Whey is a by-product of cheese production. It is an aqueous liquid rich in proteins, which, like other proteins, are broken down by the body's digestive system and converted into amino acids. These proteins do not provide a health advantage compared to other proteins already present in our diets.

Xerophilous microorganism

Microorganism able to grow at low Aw value.

ACKNOWLEDGMENTS

One can achieve more with the support of friends! It gives a shot in the arm and boosts motivation for even better results. I was once again able to experience this when writing this book.

First off, I extend a special word of gratitude to *Nelly*, my best friend and wife, for her endless patience and for sacrificing all our free time over the years and to support me while I wrote my books in a positive and comfortable environment.

I also want to thank *Dirk De Schepper* and Frederic Mortier, bioengineers in chemistry and food technology, for their significant contribution in checking and updating the technical information in this book.

Many thanks also to my loyal sponsors who ensured that the entire concept was financially feasible:
- *Pierre Bach*, owner of PCB Creatio, world leader in the area of decoration material and aids for chocolatiers (www.pcb-creation.fr)
- *Alain Boiron*, owner of Boiron, supplier of high-quality fruit pastes (www.lesvergersboiron.com)
- *Gérard* and *Dominique Dufour* of Robot Coupe Belgium, distributor of high-quality professional blenders (www.robot-coupe.be)
- *Jozef Van Elven* of Moldart, producer of all manner of equipment for chocolatiers (www.moldart.be)

I am particularly grateful to *Frank Croes* for the many years of pleasant collaboration and the wonderful photographs he took for my last five books.

And lastly, the friendly relationship with and support by the staff at Lannoo Publishing, under the expert leadership of *Johan Ghysels*, were of the utmost importance to me.

Many thanks, my friends!

Jean-Pierre Wybauw

www.lannoo.com

If you register on our website, we will send you regular newsletters
with information on new books as well as interesting and exclusive offers.

Texts: Jean-Pierre Wybauw
Photography: Frank Croes
Design: Keppie & Keppie
Translation: Lyrco

Should you have comments or questions, please contact
our editorial staff: redactielifestyle@lannoo.com

© Uitgeverij Lannoo nv, Tielt, 2010
D/2010/45/408 – NUR 441
ISBN: 978-90-209-9020-1